WEST ACADEMIC PUBLISHING'S LAW SCHOOL ADVISORY BOARD

LAWYERS, CLIENTS, AND MORAL RESPONSIBILITY

Third Edition

■ ■ ■

Jerome M. Organ
Bakken Professor of Law
University of St. Thomas School of Law

Thomas L. Shaffer
Robert E. & Marion D. Short Professor of Law, Emeritus
University of Notre Dame

Robert F. Cochran Jr.
Louis D. Brandeis Professor of Law, Emeritus
Pepperdine University

AMERICAN CASEBOOK SERIES®

WEST ACADEMIC

860 Blue Gentian Road, Suite 350
Eagan, MN 55121
1-877-888-1330

Published in the United States of America

ISBN: 979-8-88786-956-8

For Tom Shaffer (1934–2019), our co-author, friend, and mentor.

PREFACE TO THE THIRD EDITION

It has been 15 years since the Second Edition of "Lawyers, Clients, and Moral Responsibility" and 30 years since the First Edition. Authors of traditional legal textbooks prepare new editions of their works more often than this, but it may be that moral insight and how moral insight might apply to lawyers develops a little slower than courts resolve cases and legislatures pass statutes—the material of most legal textbooks.

The particular event that sparks the publication of this edition is the ABA's adoption of Standard 303(b)(3), a new requirement that law schools do more to foster "Professional Identity Formation."[1] As indicated in Interpretation 303–5: "Professional identity focuses on what it means to be a lawyer and the special obligations lawyers have to their clients and society."[2] As we explain in the Introduction to this book, professional identity formation occurs throughout a lawyer's career, in law school, law firms, bar associations, and courts (and perhaps from reading books about the legal profession and being a lawyer!) Our hope is that this book will foster professional identity formation through a focus on the moral implications of the relationship between clients and lawyers and the impact of that relationship on clients, lawyers, third parties, communities, and courts. These are important aspects of professional identity formation.

Tom Shaffer (1934–2019), one of the co-authors of this book, was one of the pioneers of the study of professional identity formation—though he

---

[1] The ABA House of Delegates approved the addition of Standard 303(b)(3) and Interpretation 303–5 at its meeting on February 14, 2022. Standard 303(b) provides as follows: "A law school shall provide substantial opportunities to students for: (1) law clinics or field placement(s); (2) student participation in pro bono legal services, including law-related public service activities; and *(3) the development of a professional identity*." (Emphasis added.) STANDARDS & RULES OF PROC. FOR APPROVAL OF LAW SCHOOLS, Standard 303(b)(3) and Interpretation 303–5 (Am. Bar Ass'n. Section of Leg. Educ. & Admissions to the Bar 2024–25) [hereinafter Standard 303(b)(3)].

[2] Interpretation 303–5 states:

> Professional identity focuses on what it means to be a lawyer and the special obligations lawyers have to their clients and society. The development of professional identity should involve an intentional exploration of the values, guiding principles, and well-being practices considered foundational to successful legal practice. Because developing a professional identity requires reflection and growth over time, students should have frequent opportunities for such development during each year of law school and in a variety of courses and co-curricular and professional development activities.

Id. at Interpretation 303–5. Notably, the ABA Standards provide no more specific delineation of the "special obligations" or the "values [and] guiding principles . . . considered foundational to successful legal practice." A recent article by one of the authors (along with several coauthors) explores these values and principles, leaning significantly on the language in the Preamble to the Model Rules. Neil W. Hamilton, Jerome M. Organ, David Grenardo, Louis D. Bilionis, Barbara Glesner Fines and Kendall Kerew, *Standard 303 and the Development of Student Professional Identity: A Framework for the Intentional Exploration of the Profession's Core Values*, 20 U. ST. THOMAS L. J. 1001 (2024).

probably never used that term. In fifteen books and over 300 articles, book chapters, and book reviews, Tom explored nearly every aspect of the legal profession. Tom's wife Mary served as a paralegal at the legal clinic at Notre Dame for many years and did a detailed edit of the first two editions of this book. We have relieved her of editing responsibilities in this edition (though we are sure it will suffer for it).[3]

Jerry Organ joins this Third Edition as a co-author. For nearly a decade, he has been the co-director of the Holloran Center for Ethical Leadership in the Professions at the University of St Thomas School of Law. Jerry brings a wealth of experience in law practice, law teaching, and mentoring law students and lawyers. Like your other authors, he has spent most of his life forming professionals.

In the years since the Second Edition of this book, earlier trends in the legal profession have continued at an increasing pace. Law firms have grown exponentially—both in personnel and in areas of service—and technology has greatly expanded the ability of lawyers (and non-lawyers) to offer legal services. Lawyers have increasingly begun to telecommute, especially since the Covid outbreak. AI has presented opportunities and risks for clients and lawyers. Each of these developments tests the moral influence lawyers and clients might have over one another, as well as the ability of senior lawyers to mentor new lawyers.

Other developments in law practice during the last 15 years create new opportunities for moral discourse between clients and lawyers. Zoom calls are better than telephone calls (though nothing beats in-person interaction with a client). Emerging forms of dispute resolution present new opportunities for clients and lawyers. Chapter Four discusses Collaborative Practice, a form of dispute resolution that is becoming especially popular in family cases. Chapter Seven discusses Restorative Justice, a form of dispute resolution in criminal cases that can yield justice, heal wounds, and even reconcile victims and defendants.

Readers of previous editions of this textbook will notice that the lawyer model discussed in Chapter One—the lawyer who controls moral choices during representation and ignores the interests of other people—is no longer "The Godfather." Though "The Godfather" movies remain at the top of lists of the best movies ever made, "The Godfather" image is not as well known as it once was. It is also a masculine image, and as you will see, the temptations described in Chapter One that yield this lawyer are experienced by both men and women. Our "Godfather" lawyer is now "The Autocrat." In this edition, "The Autocrat" lawyer controls moral choices during representation and ignores the interests of other people. The lawyer

---

[3] *See also* Robert F. Cochran, Jr., *Lawyers, Religious Faith, and Virtues: Reflections on Tom and Nancy Shaffer*, 10 ST. MARY'S J. LEGAL MALPRACTICE & ETHICS xviii (2020). Available at: https://commons.stmarytx.edu/cgi/viewcontent.cgi?article=1042&context=lmej.

models in Chapters Two through Four remain the Hired Gun, the Guru, and the Friend.

The lawyer-client relationship remains at the heart of law practice. During legal representation, the moral values of the client, the moral values of the lawyer, and the moral values underlying the legal system come into contact (and at times conflict) with one another. Whether legal representation works for the good of the client, the lawyer, third parties, and the community, will depend, in large part, on how the client and lawyer navigate that relationship. We hope this book will influence those relationships for good.

PREFACE TO THE SECOND EDITION

It has been 15 years since the publication of the first edition of *Lawyers, Clients, and Moral Responsibility*. During the time since its publication, we have had the benefit of insights from numerous reviewers, panelists, and friends. Most importantly, our students have pressed us to develop the meaning of our theory of lawyering for the very real-world legal problems they will face (and many now face). In this second edition we attempt to address many of those concerns.

Some of our students complained that our first edition had too many old stories from old novels about old lawyers. Though we think that there is much to be learned from old lawyers and old novels, we seek to update our list of stories a bit and we present a few more modern lawyers in big city, corporate law settings. We bid a fond farewell to William Faulkner's Gavin Stevens and client Lucas Beauchamp (*Intruder in the Dust*) and Anthony Trollope's Sir Abraham Haphazard and client Septimus Harding (*The Warden*). We welcome insights into corporate law practice of stories from our friends Teresa Collett (Chapter Three) and Tom Bost (Chapter Four).

Several commentators and students expressed concern that the lawyer we propose—the lawyer as friend—may inadvertently impose her values on the client, that she will be more of a guru lawyer than a friend. In Chapter Four, we add new material on "Overcoming the Unequal Power of the Law Office." We seek to suggest a method that will avoid the risk of overcoming the weaker client, while not ignoring the importance of challenging the strong client.

Finally, our friend John DiPippa noted that in the first edition's chapter on "Justice," we dealt primarily with the place of corrective justice in the lives of lawyers and clients, and paid little attention to the importance of distributive or social justice. In Chapter Seven of the new edition, we seek to remedy that with a look at the place of social justice in the law practice of Louis Brandeis.

We look forward to the insights that our friends and students will give us upon the publication of this new edition.

PREFACE TO THE FIRST EDITION

The earliest ethical tradition among American lawyers depended on a sensitive and learned moral stance in the lawyer. The grandfather of American legal ethics, David Hoffman of Baltimore, in his "Resolutions on Professional Deportment" (1836), described the beginning law student as "a young man of the soundest morals, and of the most urbane, and honourable deportment." All it was necessary for legal education to add were "a few rules for his future government." Hoffman's rules mixed regulation and morals, and claimed for the lawyer both moral leadership in the law office and stern rejection of immoral purposes in clients. Hoffman said:

> If I am satisfied from the evidence that the fact is against my client, he must excuse me if I do not see it as he does, and do not press it and should the principle [the client depends on] be at variance with sound law, it would be dishonourable folly in me to endeavor to incorporate it into the jurisprudence of the country.[1]

For Hoffman, there was a place in the practice of law for the lawyer's morality, but little place for the client's morality.[2]

It remained perhaps for the mid-twentieth century to temper this sense of aristocratic leadership with the realization that it is possible that a lawyer's client may have as much moral sensitivity as the lawyer. Modern teaching on legal counseling has borrowed as an aspiration for legal counselors the moral direction suggested by the late Carl Rogers, a humanistic psychologist:

> To be of assistance to you I will put aside myself. . . and enter into your world of perception as completely as I am able. I will become, in a sense, another self for you. . . a safe opportunity for you to discern yourself more clearly, to experience yourself more truly and deeply, to choose more significantly.[3]

For Rogers (and his counselor-at-law followers) there may be a place for the client's morality, but little place for the lawyer's morality.[4]

The Watergate break-in and cover-up in the early 1970s brought to professional and public attention the fact that some lawyers are scoundrels and that many lawyers are so in thrall to the purposes of their clients that

---

1 David Hoffman, *Resolutions in Regard to Professional Deportment*, in A Course of Legal Study (2nd ed. 1836), reprinted in Thomas L. Shaffer, American Legal Ethics: Text, Readings, and Discussion Topics 59–164 (1985) (hereinafter "American Legal Ethics").

2 *See infra* Chapter 3.

3 Carl R. Rogers, Client Centered Therapy 35 (1965).

4 *See infra* Chapter 2.

they lose their own moral identity. Watergate caused legal educators and members of the organized bar to examine the possibilities and problems that the traditions of Hoffman and Rogers present to lawyers.

One of many responses to Watergate was the suggestion from the organized bar that courts require law students to study "professional responsibility" and take court-administered examinations on legal ethics. Most states adopted a form of the A.B.A.'s Model Rules of Professional Conduct (1983), a set of rules for lawyers that is more like a criminal code than the mixture of regulation and morals of Hoffman's *Resolutions* and the lawyer codes that preceded the Model Rules. The Model Rules set aside the consensus statements of moral aspiration of the earlier codes and provide rules with which lawyers *must* comply. The Model Rules set minimum standards. Where the old lawyer standards defined the good lawyer, the new ones define the bad one. Most law school professional responsibility courses focus on the Model Rules and on appellate opinions dealing with lawyer discipline and legal malpractice. The bar examinations on professional responsibility focus entirely on lawyer disciplinary rules.

These manifestations of professional self-discipline are important, but it seems to us that so much attention is paid to the rules that minimum standards are becoming the only standards for the profession; the danger is that they will become the norm. We think that lawyers focus on the minimum standards at the expense of the morality Hoffman took for granted in lawyers and Rogers sought to discover in clients. If rules of lawyer discipline and malpractice are the only or the primary limit on what lawyers and clients do, we are in trouble.

Our purposes in this book are to seek out and examine the moral standards clients and their lawyers bring to the law office,[5] to hold those standards up as better than the minimum lawyer standards, and to identify a way that lawyers and clients can talk about and apply their standards in the law office on ordinary Wednesday afternoons.[6]

---

5 *See infra* Chapters 6–9.

6 *See infra* Chapters 4 and 5.

Acknowledgements

We thank Dean Ken Starr, Dean Ronald Phillips, and Grant Nelson for their support and encouragement in this project along with our current deans, Dean Paul Caron and Dean Dan Kelly. We also thank the following for their suggestions and comments: Joe Allegretti, Bob Destro, Eileen Doran, Nancy Magnusson Fagan, Rus Gough, James Davidson Hunter, Sandy Levinson, John Leubsdorf, Sharon Marshall, Morris Miller, Greg Ogden, Jim Ostenson, Mike Raichelson, Ed Rubin, Barb Ryan, Jack Sammons, Judith Schmidt, Nancy Shaffer, LaGard Smith, Jim Sorenson, Beat Steiner, and Ellen Thorne. Melissa Thornsberry, Jeff Wyss, Pamela Davidson, Joe ElGuindy, Eric Messelt, Candace Warren, Sophia Sipsas, Jeanne Pepper, Stephen Middlebrook and John Selbak provided assistance with research and Dorothy Aiken, Linda Harrington, and Dorothy Olbricht provided assistance in manuscript preparation.

We are indebted as well to the following authors and publishers who gave us permission to reprint substantial portions of their work:

Teresa Stanton Collett, *To Be a Professing Woman,* in Can a Good Christian Be a Good Lawyer?: Homilies, Witnesses, and Reflections, pp. 56–59 (Thomas E. Baker & Timothy W. Floyd eds., 1998). Copyright © by University of Notre Dame Press. Reprinted with permission.

Rand Jack and Dana Crowley Jack, *Moral Vision and Professional Decisions: The Changing Values of Women and Men Lawyers*, pp. 89–92. Copyright © Cambridge University Press 1989. Reprinted with the permission of Cambridge University Press.

Reed Elizabeth Loder, *Out From Uncertainty: A Model of the Lawyer-Client Relationship*, 2 S. Cal. Interdisc. L.J. 89, 127–28 (1993). Copyright © by Southern California Interdisciplinary Law Journal. Reprinted with permission.

John T. Noonan, Jr., *Distinguished Alumni Lecture—Other People's Morals: The Lawyer's Conscience*, pp. 234–35. The full text of this article originally appeared at 48 Tenn. L. Rev. 227 (1981) and may be obtained from the Business Manager, Tennessee Law Review Association, Inc., 1505 W. Cumberland, Knoxville, TN 37996–1800. Copyright © by the Tennessee Law Review. Reprinted with permission.

Steven Wexler, *Practicing Law for Poor People*, pp. 1063–1064 (1970). Reprinted by permission of The Yale Law Journal Company and Fred B. Rothman & Company from *The Yale Law Journal*, Vol. 79, pp. 1049–1067. Copyright © by the Yale Law Journal.

Summary of Contents

TABLE OF CONTENTS

LAWYERS, CLIENTS, AND MORAL RESPONSIBILITY

Third Edition

INTRODUCTION

■ ■ ■

Lawyers provide an important service to the clients they represent and to the communities in which they practice. They speak in all sorts of contexts on behalf of clients who don't know the language of the law.[1] They help clients put together deals that employ people and get goods and services to other people. Lawyers help clients settle the vast majority of cases before trial. When cases cannot be resolved and go to trial, having neutral judges decide the dispute is vastly preferable to the violent alternatives to which parties might otherwise turn. Lawyers assist judges, juries, mediators, and clients, as they wrestle with notions of justice, mercy, and truthfulness.

Lawyers carry a special responsibility for the rule of law. Prosecutors and judges punish law-breakers and deter future crimes. Criminal defense lawyers protect defendants' rights and restrain prosecutors who might otherwise abuse their authority. Plaintiffs' lawyers require people who commit torts and breach contracts to compensate those people they have harmed. Defense lawyers make sure plaintiffs' lawyers prove their case. Business lawyers "enforce" the law by advising clients to comply with the law. They engage in conflict prevention before anyone else has even considered the possibility of conflict, drafting partnership agreements, sales agreements, articles of incorporation, and wills with an eye toward avoiding future conflicts. People tend to take the rule of law for granted, but a visit to a country where the rule of law has broken down will cause you to hug the first lawyer you encounter on your return. Lawyers' work enables people to thrive.

But the law can be used to harm people and lawyers can cause harm to their clients and to others through the way they conduct themselves as professionals. The Model Rules of Professional Conduct are designed to regulate lawyer behavior so that the clients of lawyers are rarely harmed. But even while serving their clients in accordance with the Model Rules of Professional Conduct, lawyers may cause harm to others—those who experience collateral damage as a result of the adversarial process.

The question raised by this book is how clients and lawyers will determine what lawyers will do and say on behalf of clients. That, ideally, is a question for thoughtful client/lawyer counseling conversations.

---

[1] Jack L. Sammons, *Rank Strangers to Me: Shaffer and Cochran's Friendship Model of Moral Counseling in the Law Office*, 18 U. ARK. LITTLE ROCK L. J. 1, 44 (1995).

Law office conversations are almost always moral conversations. This is so because they involve law, and law is a claim that people make on one another. The moral content is often implicit, but it is always there. Legal claims rest on normative considerations as well as objective rules. And when clients and/or their lawyers make a decision to take advantage of the rules, they are deciding to do something when they might have decided they ought not to. If it is possible for a serious conversation between a lawyer and a client in a law office to be without moral content, we cannot think of an example.[2]

Moral decisions during legal representation are important for several reasons. First, almost all decisions made in the law office will benefit some people at the expense of others. Will the client assert or resist a claim? In a divorce, will the client take actions that will harm a child or spouse? In structuring a business deal, or writing a will, who will benefit? Who will lose? Will the officers of a corporation consider the effects of its actions on workers, on consumers, on competitors, on the environment, on the community? The heart of the moral and religious teaching of most North Americans is that there is value to other people. As Justice James Wilson put it, the human person is "the noblest work of God."[3] Moral choices in legal representation are important because they affect other people and people are important.

Second, moral decisions during legal representation are important for the sake of the client and lawyer who make them. For most people, the obligation to act morally is a matter of obedience to their conscience and to their God. The moral teachings of our traditions concerning justice, mercy, reconciliation, use of wealth, stewardship of creation, and truthfulness speak directly to many of the issues involved in legal representation. Legal representation provides the lawyer and the client the opportunity to become better people.

Third, and maybe less obviously, the exercise of morality in the law office is important because it helps to preserve freedom from domination by the government and others. The law regulates some aspects of social morality; it tells us how we may and may not treat others in certain contexts. But it leaves a great deal of morality to individual choice, to personal habit, and to the moral authority of voluntary communities, giving each of us the opportunity to do good and to become better. If clients and lawyers merely make the selfish choice when faced with moral issues during legal representation, the only morality that places limits on what

---

[2] *See* Thomas L. Shaffer, *The Practice of Law as Moral Discourse*, 55 NOTRE DAME LAWYER 231, 232 (1979); *see also* Robert K. Vischer, *Legal Advice as Moral Perspective*, 19 GEORGETOWN J. LEGAL ETHICS 225 (2006).

[3] *Chisholm v. Georgia*, 2 U.S. 419, 463 (1793). The full quote from the opinion written by Justice James Wilson reads as follow: "A state I cheerfully fully admit, is the noblest work of Man. But, Man himself, free and honest, is, I speak as to this world, the noblest work of God."

they do is that imposed by the law. If law becomes the only limitation on human action, the state will either leave people to be uncivil toward one another, or intrude into more and more aspects of human life.

Edmund Burke said that he would be guided by "not what a lawyer tells me I may do; but what humanity, reason, and justice, tell me I ought to do."[4] It is our hope that clients will get assistance in determining what they "may do" *and* what they "ought to do" in their lawyers' offices.

With the growth of computer programming and artificial intelligence, the legal profession no longer has a monopoly on telling clients what the law says about whether they can do or can't do something. Many "clients" get their legal advice over the internet. One space where lawyers as professionals continue to provide added value to their clients that probably can't be provided electronically is facilitating normative conversations—helping clients make decisions about what they should do that are meaningful to the clients given their value systems and faith traditions.

Many law students and lawyers ask, "Can I be a lawyer and a good person?" One way a lawyer can be a good person is by helping the client who wants to know, "Can I be your client and a good person?" This book is concerned with how a client and lawyer can decide what they ought to do. It engages this issue by helping law students think about who they want to be as lawyers; about the way in which they want to interact with clients to serve their clients well. Accordingly, this book is about professional identity formation—who law students want to be as lawyers.

Part One identifies four models of lawyer-client interactions and the extent to which those models engage moral concerns. The fourth model presents a method of lawyer-client deliberation that may enable lawyers and clients to notice and resolve moral issues more intentionally and more appropriately for the benefit of the client and other people who might be affected. Part Two discusses substantive moral values that might inform lawyer-client discourse and actions.

---

[4] *Quoted in* Geoffrey C. Hazard, Jr., Ethics in the Practice of Law 1 (1978).

PART ONE

FOUR APPROACHES TO MORAL ISSUES IN LEGAL REPRESENTATION

■ ■ ■

We first look at four stories about lawyers and clients that illustrate different approaches to the moral content in legal representation. The stories involve different types of legal problems arising in the context of distinct models of lawyer-client interactions. But they all raise the most common moral issue that arises in law practice: whether the lawyer and client should take actions that will work to the disadvantage of other people. In these stories, as in law practice, the right answers to some moral issues are clear; the right answers to others are not.

We can analyze the way lawyers approach moral issues with clients by asking two questions: (1) Who controls the representation? and (2) Are the interests of those other than the client taken into consideration? Each of the models of interaction presented in these stories represents a common form of lawyer-client interaction that is shaped by a different combination of answers to these questions. We suggest a metaphor for each lawyer.

In the first story, when the client consults the attorney, the attorney usurps decision-making authority from the client and unilaterally makes the choices the lawyer feels will help the client (and the lawyer) find "success"—however the lawyer defines success given the circumstances. The lawyer acts as an "Autocrat"—an authoritarian decision-maker who takes little account of concerns about client autonomy or about how the lawyer's decisions might affect other people. This is attorney control with no regard for moral considerations.

In the second story, the client is the decision-maker and controls the choices regarding how to proceed; the lawyer defers to the client's choices, out of a desire to honor the client's autonomy (self-rule). The lawyer acts as a "Hired Gun," at the direction of the client, without regard for how the actions taken may affect or injure other people. This is client control with no regard from the attorney for moral considerations. (The client may or may not have moral considerations that influence the client's choices, but they are not integrated into the lawyer-client interaction because the lawyer focuses solely on client autonomy with no consideration of moral concerns.)

In the third story, the client turns the case over to the lawyer and defers to the lawyer's determination about how to proceed. In this model, however, the lawyer tries to find the morally correct choice. While the lawyer shows little concern for client autonomy, the lawyer does show concern for how decisions may affect other people and wants the client to do the "right" thing. But it is the "right" thing in the lens of the lawyer's sense of morality. The lawyer acts as a "Guru" making the moral choices for the client who allows the lawyer to exercise authority over decision-making. This is attorney control based on the attorney's perception of moral considerations.

In the fourth story, the lawyer and client together wrestle with and resolve the moral issues while working through the client's legal problem. They collaborate in fostering the good. The lawyer and client are both concerned with the impact of the representation on other people. The lawyer remains cognizant of the importance of client autonomy. Through the interaction the lawyer tries to help the client remain true to herself and perhaps grow as a person. The lawyer acts in a way we might expect a "Friend" of the client to act. This interaction involves explicit discussion of moral considerations but ultimately leaves to the client the responsibility for decision-making.

Exploring these four approaches to moral issues in legal representation provides an opportunity for law students to engage in professional identity formation. By engaging with these different models and reflecting on the scenarios presented, we hope law students will begin to understand who they want to be as lawyers and how they want to interact with their clients as they try to serve their clients with an appropriate concern for others.

CHAPTER 1

THE LAWYER AS AUTOCRAT[1]: LAWYER CONTROL WITHOUT REGARD FOR OTHER PEOPLE

■ ■ ■

1. THE FAMILY TRUST DISPUTE

The following is Judge John Noonan's description of a case that arose in Boston in the early 1900s:

* * *

> Mr. Warren . . . died and left a very prosperous unincorporated paper business. Mr. Warren wanted his widow and five children to have the benefit of the business [and he] set up a trust in such a way that Sam Warren, the oldest son, was one of the trustees and also manager and lessee of the plant. The arrangement was that the lessee would give a share of the trust profits to Sam and to the other four Warren children and the widow. Everything in this complicated plan hinged on the family's confidence in Sam—a confidence that existed when the trust was created. The family thought Sam was the most capable member of the family and happily turned the business over to him. Then, as sometimes happens in families, with the passage of time there was a falling out between Sam and his brother Ned. Ned was regarded as something of a dilettante, living in England and spending his share of the income on antiques. Ned resented Sam's patronizing him, and finally he began to suspect Sam of bad faith in engineering the entire arrangement. . . .
>
> [Ned's] lawyer filed a complaint in equity charging Sam with breach of trust. At the same time Ned wrote Sam a letter in which he stated:
>
>> The phrases are such as in a legal document I have felt obliged to sign, but are very far from representing my feelings

[1] In this Chapter, "The Autocrat" lawyer has replaced "The Godfather" lawyer of earlier editions of this book. This lawyer, however, remains a lawyer who controls client choices during representation and ignores the interests of other people. For an explanation of this change, see The Preface.

> toward you. . . . Let us try to agree; it would be much pleasanter.
>
> Your affectionate brother,
> E.P. Warren.
>
> In this simple letter two stages of thought are established. Ned wants to be an affectionate brother, but he also has a sense of compulsion to use harsh legal formulas. Because he is caught in the legal process, he feels he must sign the hostile document with its terrible charges. The letter shows how Ned shifted responsibility for the document to his lawyer, while his lawyer had shifted the responsibility to Ned. The upshot was both dramatic and sad. Sam was offended deeply by being accused of breach of trust when he knew he had acted in an honorable fashion. He refused to settle, and the case went to trial. Ned's first lawyer, who had given the trouble between the brothers its formal shape, engaged a formidable trial lawyer, Sherman Whipple, to conduct the trial. Sam was put on the witness stand, and of course Ned's lawyer began to dig away. After days of Whipple's keen cross-examination, Sam died. This was the tragic outcome of a client's ceasing to be a loyal brother and of a lawyer's view of himself as a depersonalized instrument of aggression.[2]
>
> * * *

We do not have an account of the conversations between Ned and his lawyers. It is likely that Ned went to his lawyers with suspicions and accusations, and that his lawyers in their roles as advocates took Ned's side and began to see and to portray Ned's brother as the enemy. Ned turned the claim over to his lawyers; they decided what to do with it, and apparently decided as advocates for what they perceived to be Ned's interest without fully exploring what Ned's interests really were. It is likely that no one made a conscious choice concerning the moral issue; no one decided that it was right to accuse Ned's brother of a breach of trust (or that it was wrong, but that they would do it anyway). The lawyer's role as advocate and the legal system were left to run their course. The result (Sam's death) is unusual, but it is a poignant example of the pain people create for one another when they go to law.

The letter Ned sent to his brother indicates that he had reservations about the decision to accuse his brother of a breach of trust, but that he followed the lead of his lawyers. The lawyers may have had less than whole-hearted support for the allegation, but they played out what they

---

[2] John T. Noonan, Jr., *Distinguished Alumni Lecture—Other People's Morals: The Lawyer's Conscience*, 48 TENN. L. REV. 234–36 (1981) (*citing Warren v. Warren*, No. 14630, Mass., *filed* Dec. 13, 1909). The case involved a will drafted by Louis D. Brandeis while he was practicing law; *see also* John P. Frank, *The Legal Ethics of Louis D. Brandeis*, 17 STAN. L. REV. 683, 694–98 (1965).

perceived to be their roles as Ned's advocates. As Judge Noonan says, "The letter shows how Ned shifted responsibility for the document to his lawyer, while his lawyer had shifted the responsibility to Ned." Ned's lawyers controlled his decisions and made them according to what they perceived to be Ned's interests. They did not comprehend that Ned's interests may have included preserving in some way Ned's relationship with his brother. Perhaps Ned failed to communicate clearly (or the lawyers failed to hear and understand) that Ned may have valued and wanted to retain a relationship with his brother.

Ned's lawyers acted in a combination of roles that is common for lawyers: they served as professionals and as advocates. Under this perception of a professional, the professional is the expert, the decision-maker. This professional is concerned with the technical problems of the client. But lawyers tend to—are trained to—view all of the issues that arise in legal representation as technical problems understood through the lens of the law.[3] And, technician-professionals tend to make most of the decisions for their technically unsophisticated clients. As advocates, Ned's lawyers pursued the interest of their client, and like most advocates, they viewed their client's interest in terms of financial success (without regard, in this case, to preserving family relationships).

A more recent example of lawyers constructing a legal defense without concern for other people is the work of the lawyers who defended the Catholic Church in the 1990s with respect to claims that priests had sexually abused minors. In a review of the sexual abuse crisis commissioned by The United States Conference of Catholic Bishops, one whole section emphasized misplaced reliance on attorneys who opted for strong advocacy that featured an aggressive litigation defense that did not contemplate the possibility of apology or of approaching the dispute in a way designed to repair the strained relationship between the institutional church and the victims.[4] The lawyers for the Catholic Church may have pursued what they thought was in the interest of the client. It did not turn out so well.

2. THE AUTOCRAT

This model of lawyer as "Autocrat" appears to be shaped partly by the sense that the lawyer is the expert—the professional technician who should be the decision-maker and to whom the client cedes decision-making authority. It also is shaped by Lord Brougham's statement describing his

---

[3] David Luban, *Paternalism and the Legal Profession*, 1981 WIS. L. REV. 454, 459 n.9 (1981) (hereinafter "*Paternalism and the Legal Profession*").

[4] *See* Vischer, *supra* Introduction note 2, at 249–54 (citing The National Review Board for the Protection of Children and Young People, A Report on the Crisis in the Catholic Church in the United States 1 (Feb. 27, 2004), available at https://www.usccb.org/sites/default/files/issues-and-action/child-and-youth-protection/upload/National-Review-Board-Report-2004.pdf at 119–20).

role as "advocate" when defending the Queen of England early in the 19th Century:

> In the discharge of his duty, [the advocate] knows but one person in all the world, and that person is his client. To save that client by all means and expedients, and at all hazards and costs to other persons, and, among them, to himself, is his first and only duty; and in performing this duty he must not regard the alarm, the torments, the destruction which he may bring upon others.[5]

The professional training law students receive reinforces this idea of advocate grounded in "technical" proficiency with disregard for others and other aspects of humanity.[6] The profound emphasis on "thinking like a lawyer" narrows the perspective of students to focus on the law or the legal issues without regard to the non-legal concerns of their clients or the concerns of others.[7]

Ned's lawyers *assumed* that their job was to go after Sam. It is not clear that Ned directed the assault; he seems to have wanted, in his letter to Sam, to say that he did not. The lawyers for the Catholic Church in the sexual abuse crisis assumed that their job was to go after the victims—to staunchly contest liability and damages in an effort to minimize the cost to the Catholic Church. It is not clear that the bishops directed this approach or would have chosen this approach if consulted. Indeed, one bishop noted:

> We made terrible mistakes. Because the attorneys said over and over "Don't talk to the victims, don't go near them," and here they were victims. I heard victims say "We would not have taken it to [our attorneys] had someone just come to us and said 'I'm sorry.' " But we listened to the attorneys.[8]

As Autocrats, Ned's lawyers controlled the action in the belief that they were serving the interests of their client. But they did so without fully understanding whether Ned really wanted them to pursue the dispute with Sam so aggressively and without regard to the harm their actions might cause to other people. Similarly, the lawyers for the Catholic Church controlled the action in the belief that an aggressive defense strategy served their client's interest. But they did so without offering their client a

---

[5] Trial of Queen Caroline 8 (1821), *quoted in* Monroe H. Freedman, Understanding Lawyers' Ethics 65–66 (1990) (hereinafter "Brougham").

[6] *See* Roger C. Cramton, *The Ordinary Religion of the Law School Classroom*, 29 J. LEGAL EDUC. 247, 258 (1978).

[7] William Sullivan, *et al.*, Educating Lawyers at 28 (Carnegie 2007)(Describing three "apprenticeships" in professional education—the first apprenticeship of cognitive knowledge and analytical skills, the second apprenticeship of practical skills, and the third apprenticeship of professional identity—and noting that in legal education the first apprenticeship ("thinking like a lawyer") profoundly shapes the third apprenticeship of professional identity.)

[8] *See* Vischer, *supra* Introduction note 2, at 249 (quoting statement from Report on the Crisis in the Catholic Church in the United States at 121).

chance to consider whether less adversarial approaches might have made more sense.

Autocrats either decide what their clients' interests are, without consulting their clients, or they persuade their clients to accept the lawyers' views on what the client's interests are. They pursue client interests with their own "technical" devices, without much interest in their clients' moral reservations or the impact of their actions on others.

3. THE AUTOCRAT AND CLIENT INTEREST: "ACQUISITIVE" PARENTALISM

In the family estate story, it appears from Ned's letter that the decision to sue was primarily that of Ned's lawyers. Ned's lawyers would argue that they acted in Ned's interest. They (as well as the Catholic Church's lawyers) acted to preserve what most lawyers think of when they think of client interest—financial success. Ned's lawyers appear to be typical of what Dr. Robert S. Redmount refers to as "acquisitive" lawyers:

> It is practically "legal instinct" to address most matters in terms of some kind of possession or benefit, and to aspire to some advantage in and over situations. In the principal aspects of a legal practice, the attorney struggles to advance or preserve property rights, to multiply or sustain economic benefits, or to facilitate economic and political power.[9]

The Autocrat lawyer seeks the client's financial benefit, without regard to harm caused to other people and without serious concern for the client's relationships—or even for what the client may really want. The Autocrat, in the words of William Simon, resolves "questions unilaterally in terms of the imputed ends of [client] selfishness."[10] Ned's lawyers saw his problem as a technical problem: how to obtain the most money for their client. They concluded that filing suit, alleging breach of trust, and aggressive cross-examination were the answers. (They may have succeeded; Sam's estate ultimately settled the case.)

The lawyers for the Catholic Church similarly saw the church's problem as a technical problem: how to limit the church's liability. They concluded that defending the claims vigorously without any apology from the Catholic Church was what their client wanted, without apparently consulting with their client fully about the client's actual interests/goals and preferences for strategy.

---

[9] Robert S. Redmount, *Attorney Personalities and Some Psychological Aspects of Legal Consultation*, 109 U. PA. L. REV. 972, 975 (1961).

[10] William H. Simon, *The Ideology of Advocacy: Procedural Justice and Professional Ethics*, 1978 WIS. L. REV. 29, 56 (1978) (hereinafter "*The Ideology of Advocacy*").

Autocrats are not only technicians; they also tend to be parental—limiting someone's freedom for the sake of his or her own good.[11] The Autocrat, who could enhance the client's freedom, restricts it in the name of serving the client's interests.

It appears that Ned's lawyers acted in what they considered to be his interests, rather than allowing him to control the representation. Similarly, the lawyers for the Catholic Church acted in what they thought were the best interests of the church without inviting church authorities to have a meaningful voice in the representation.

The parentalism in both the Warren case and the Catholic Church case is characteristic of the professional in North American culture. As Richard Wasserstrom put it, in an essay that has become a classic:

> [T]he professional often, if not systematically, interacts with the client in both a manipulative and a paternalistic fashion. . . . [F]rom the professional's point of view the client is seen and responded to more like an object than a human being, and more like a child than an adult. The professional does not, in short, treat the client like a person; the professional does not accord the client the respect that he or she deserves.[12]

Wasserstrom's description of the attorney's perspective on clients does not arise from whole cloth, but from the nature of the legal training and professional formation provided by many law schools and by mentors and by lawyers that young lawyers observe.

Lawyers may assert authority over clients directly and openly, but, as Wasserstrom notes, they may also assert authority by manipulating clients. In Austin Sarat and William Felstiner's studies of divorce lawyers' interviews with clients, they found that the common pattern was manipulation. Lawyers manipulated clients to settle by exaggerating the risks of loss.[13] They maintained control of cases by portraying law as an "insiders' game" where they had the necessary connections with public authorities. The lawyers portrayed even simple concepts of law in complex, unclear terms that clients could not understand. When trying to persuade

---

[11] *See* Dennis Thompson, *Paternalism in Medicine, Law, and Public Policy, in* Ethics Teaching in Higher Education 246 (D. Callahan & S. Bok eds., 1980), *quoted in* Luban, *Paternalism and the Legal Profession, supra* Chapter 1 note 3, at 461 (We use parentalism rather than paternalism in an effort to be more gender neutral.)

[12] Richard Wasserstrom, *Lawyers as Professionals: Some Moral Issues*, 5 HUM. RTS. 1, 19 (1975).

[13] Austin Sarat & William L. F. Felstiner, Divorce Lawyers and Their Clients 57 (1995). Since the 1990s, new models of lawyering have gained traction in family law—including collaborative lawyering—which reflects a profoundly different conception of the engagement between lawyer and client and the opposing party and the opposing party's lawyer. *See* Robert F. Cochran, Jr., *Legal Ethics and Collaborative Practice Ethics*, 38 HOFSTRA L. REV. 537–567 (2009) in Hofstra Collaborative Law Symposium (hereinafter "*Collaborative Practice Ethics*").

clients, "[t]hey construct[ed] meanings in the service of [their own] power."[14]

Autocrats might argue, much like a mother or father, that they know better than their clients what will be in their clients' best interests. At times a client may be irrational, but in general we do not think that it is the place of the lawyer to be a parent to the client. We would rarely argue that the lawyer should override the client's values. As David Luban puts it, "[V]alues are definitive of the person" and, therefore, "attempting to . . . override them directly assaults the integrity of his or her personality."[15] Parentalism does not provide sufficient respect for the client's mind and conscience. Parentalism assaults the client's dignity and usurps client autonomy.

Not only does lawyer parentalism show insufficient respect for the client, it is likely that the lawyer does not know what is best. Client involvement in decision-making is likely to provide more satisfying results to the client than attorney control. Clients are likely to be better judges of their own interests than their lawyers. Even if we were to judge legal representation according to financial benefit alone, empirical evidence indicates that client control yields better results than lawyer control, and that client-lawyer partnership yields the best results.[16] Moreover, recent empirical research shows that clients frequently are frustrated and dissatisfied when lawyers act arrogantly, dictate the outcome, and fail to listen to clients.[17]

When lawyers are not only parental but focus almost exclusively on client legal interests or financial interests, we have not merely lawyers as parents, but lawyers as bad parents. The lawyer not only dominates but leads clients to focus narrowly on legal issues or to follow their most selfish instincts. This suggests there is a significant "alignment" problem between the Autocrat lawyer and perhaps a significant number of her clients who want to be heard and want to have a voice in deciding how to proceed, but are shut out by the Autocrat. Even if they end up satisfied with the result,

---

[14] Sarat & Felstiner, *supra* Chapter 1 note 13 at 146.

[15] Luban, *Paternalism and the Legal Profession, supra* Chapter 1 note 3, at 471; *see generally id.* at 473.

[16] *See* Douglas Rosenthal, Lawyer and Client: Who's in Charge 38–59 (1974); Robert F. Cochran, Jr., *Legal Representatives and the Next Steps Toward Client Control: Attorney Malpractice for the Failure to Allow the Client to Control Negotiation and Pursue Alternatives to Litigation*, 47 WASH. & LEE L. REV. 819, 833–36 (1990) (hereinafter "*Legal Representatives and Client Control*").

[17] Clark D. Cunningham, *What Do Clients Want from Their Lawyers?*, 2013 J. DISP. RESOL. 143 (2013) (citing empirical research from Australia and England highlighting that clients frequently are dissatisfied because their lawyers did not listen to them, did not respect them and lacked empathy). One of your authors has students interview satisfied and dissatisfied clients as a class assignment. Over several years, dissatisfied clients consistently expressed frustration and dissatisfaction because their attorneys didn't listen to them, dictated the outcome, and were arrogant and not empathetic. Results on file with author.

they well may be very dissatisfied with the process—with the nature of the service they received.[18]

4. THE LAWYER AS ADVOCATE: THE GOOD-OF-THE-SYSTEM ARGUMENT

If they were accused of causing harm to Sam Warren, Ned's lawyers would be likely to respond with a "role morality" argument. Lawyers for the Catholic Church likely would make similar claims. They would likely argue that their responsibilities as lawyer—or even the very notion of being a lawyer—assign them the narrow role of advocate.[19]

We are troubled when the system calls on a lawyer to play a role that is inconsistent with the person the lawyer is. Playing a role is, by definition, inconsistent with authenticity. There are two moral arguments for carrying out the role of advocate: One is that lawyer advocacy is good for the legal system. The other (which we will discuss in the next chapter) is that lawyer advocacy is good for the client.

The argument that the adversary system will work for the good of the legal system is based on a courtroom model: If both sides are represented by aggressive advocates, the judge or jury will hear the strongest arguments for each side and will be able to decide wisely. This argument rests on a social-Darwinian confidence—a faith—that the just claim will survive because the judge or jury is able to decide what is best.

Murray Schwartz has identified two vocational principles that follow from this good-of-the-system argument for the lawyer's role as advocate: (1) the principle of professionalism—the lawyer must act to "maximize the likelihood that the client will prevail" and (2) the principle of nonaccountability—"[w]hen acting as an advocate for a client according to the Principle of Professionalism, a lawyer is neither legally, professionally, nor morally accountable for the means used or the ends achieved."[20]

No doubt the adversary system is effective at times in assisting judges and juries. Judges are much more likely to feel confident in their decisions when they have had effective, aggressive advocates on each side. But this functional view of partisan advocacy assumes that what is good for the

---

[18] *Id.*

[19] *See* Brougham, *supra* Chapter 1 note 5; Michael Ariens, *Brougham's Ghost*, 35 N. ILL. U. L. REV. 263, 312–14 (2015)(describing historical context in which Brougham's statement came to represent the nature of the zealous advocate); *but see* Kendall Kerew, *The Rule of Law, The Lawyer's Role as a Public Citizen, and Professional Identity: How Fostering the Development of Professional Identity Can Help Law Schools Address the Crisis Facing American Democracy*, 75 MERCER L. REV. 1449, 1459–62 (2024)(noting that the Preamble to the Model Rules of Professional Conduct highlights three roles of a lawyer—representative of clients, officer of the court, and public citizen with a special responsibility for the quality of justice—and that law schools have to do more to help graduates appreciate all three roles).

[20] Murray Schwartz, *The Professionalism and Accountability of Lawyers*, 66 CAL. L. REV. 669, 673 (1978).

judiciary is good for the community. And it tends to ignore the effects that advocacy, even at its best, has on the parties and on other people. The adversary system may have worked "effectively" in Ned's case: Wealthy clients, effective lawyers, and several days in court may have led to a fair settlement of the underlying dispute. But a common result of litigation even when judges and juries make wise decisions and the parties survive the ordeal, is that the parties are angry with each other, often more angry than they were before they came to visit their lawyers. Their relationships have been made worse in "the administration of justice." Losers in court may value that they had their day in court, but may feel that there were ways in which the system worked to their disadvantage. Winners, in spite of having a favorable result, may be angry that they had to pay so much to get what they deserved all along.

In addition, many of the people who are affected by legal decisions are not in court and do not have advocates to argue their positions. By the time of Ned Warren's lawsuit, the Warren family was spread over three generations, and the Warren business had hundreds of employees and customers. Sam's death and the settlement of the case after Sam's death affected all of them. Legal decisions that are sound as to the parties may work to the detriment of those who are not represented. Litigation is likely to cause collateral damage.

Finally, the model put forth by supporters of partisan advocacy—well-prepared and effective advocates on each side and an effective judge and jury—is an ideal case. In many cases, the adversary system does not work so well. Often the parties do not have equal resources and lawyers do not have equal abilities. One side is not as well represented as the other. Or one side may not be represented at all; most people in North America cannot afford protracted services from a lawyer and an increasing number are representing themselves pro se. Even when both lawyers are effective advocates, the judge or jury may be ineffective.

Whether or not the good-of-society argument for lawyer advocacy makes sense in the courtroom, lawyer advocacy makes little sense in the law office. In the office, there is no neutral third party to choose between the arguments of advocates;[21] the lawyer and client determine what to do. The state is only dimly present as a source of justice. In the law office, justice is something people give to one another. If, in the law office, there is justification for taking the selfish action, it cannot be because the state, as arbiter of what is just, points the way.

There is clearly a place for lawyer advocacy, even aggressive lawyer advocacy. Lawyers have battled the evils of our society—the fight for racial

[21] *See id.* at 677–78.

desegregation comes to mind[22]—and lawyers have represented clients who were being abused, who desperately needed aggressive representation. Lawyers speak for those who would have a hard time speaking the language of the law for themselves. Aggressive advocacy on each side can aid judges and juries in making decisions. But the fact that there is a place for advocacy does not mean that lawyers can put blinders on and assume both that aggressive advocacy is routinely appropriate and that aggressive advocacy can be pursued with a moral license to harm other people.

Lawyers may not know enough about the interests of all of those who will be affected by legal action to "guarantee real fairness"[23] (no one does), but lawyers and clients are likely to know a lot about the people involved in a lawsuit (much more than the judges and juries). Often lawyers and clients are able to talk about what is fair—if they want to—and to decide what is fair. We suggest that lawyers have a moral responsibility for what they know and for what they do. This responsibility is complicated by the additional responsibility (also a moral responsibility) that lawyers have to clients, but lawyers should not hide from the complications of the moral life behind the illusion that the adversary system will always yield the just result.

The issue is not whether moral soundness in life is easy. Determining the directions indicated by justice and mercy may be difficult; often, in the words of Charles Wolfram, "the paths of right and wrong conduct do not clearly stretch out from one's feet."[24] We do not suggest that the moral life is an easy life, nor even that the moral life can be lived without harm.

5. LAW SCHOOL TRAINING IN PROFESSIONAL ADVOCACY

It is our sense that Autocrats, who pursue their sense of "client victory," regardless of the effects on other people, and, at times, regardless of the deepest wishes of their clients, get their start in law school. Students are taught to think of themselves as advocates in law school, when they have no clients to suggest limits on their advocacy. When they graduate, serving as advocates is what they believe they are expected to do: clients are occasions of advocacy. Law students are not trained to worry about the desires, beliefs, and relationships of clients.[25] When they counsel clients, they tend to counsel clients to want what advocates are trained to get.

---

[22] *See* Richard Kluger, Simple Justice: The History of *Brown v. Board of Education* and Black America's Struggle for Equality (3d ed. 2004).

[23] Thomas D. Morgan, *Thinking About Lawyers As Counselors,* 42 FLA. L. REV. 439, 453 (1990).

[24] Charles W. Wolfram, Modern Legal Ethics 71 (1986).

[25] *See* Cramton, *supra* Chapter 1 note 6, at 261–62.

This professional identity formation reality was illuminated in the book *Educating Lawyers*. In discussing the three apprenticeships associated with professional training—the cognitive/analytical, the practical skills, and professional identity formation—the authors of *Educating Lawyers* noted that law schools are very strong on the first apprenticeship of "thinking like a lawyer," and have been paying more attention to the second apprenticeship of practical skills, but that the third apprenticeship of professional identity formation has been undernourished and shaped largely by the profound emphasis on "thinking like a lawyer."[26] As a result, the law student experience is one in which the lawyer's role as legal technician and advocate gets emphasized at the expense of attention to clients and morality.[27]

Here is a small example of the tendencies of law students and their teachers.[28] Each year, the American Bar Association sponsors several national advocacy tournaments involving law students. Most involve trial or appellate advocacy. One is the client counseling competition. (It may be that the trial and appellate advocacy tournaments attract the more aggressive students. If so, our story is the more troubling. And it is a perennial irony of the client counseling movement, which had its start in Louis M. Brown's concern for training law students in law office skills, that legal counselors-in-training are invited to compete against one another.)

Many years ago, the final round of the ABA's client counseling competition involved a client who lived with his girlfriend. She was pregnant and wanted, in the language of the day, "to keep her baby." The young man came to see a lawyer about what he should do. He began his interview by indicating (perhaps no more than hinting) that he wanted to be fair to his girlfriend and to accept his responsibilities toward his child. This signal could be comparable to indications from Ned Warren that he wanted to maintain the family relationship and not be too adversarial. Just as Ned Warren's signal fell on deaf ears, so did this young man's concerns fall on deaf ears in the ABA trial competition.

None of the student teams—not one—seemed to hear that murmur of conscience in their client. None perceived the possibility of what Stanley Hauerwas has called "the triumph of meaning over power,"[29] that is, the triumph of conscience over the chance that the law would let this young man neglect this young woman and their child. The judges of the final round, all distinguished lawyers, hardly mentioned the point. Instead the young man's lawyers, the best that American law schools produced that year to be counselors-at-law, *and their judges*, talked about influencing the

[26] See Sullivan, *et al.*, Educating Lawyers, *supra* Chapter 1 note 7.

[27] See Cramton, *supra* Chapter 1 note 6, at 261–62.

[28] *See* Louis M. Brown & Thomas L. Shaffer, *Toward a Jurisprudence for the Law Office*, 17 AM. J. OF JURISPRUDENCE 125 (1972).

[29] *See* Stanley Hauerwas, Truthfulness and Tragedy (1977).

girlfriend toward abortion, about litigating the issue of paternity (an issue the client had not raised), and about minimizing his financial responsibilities to his girlfriend and their child. These lawyers-in-training were well on the way to becoming Autocrats. It seemed as if conscience had no place in a law office, not even when the client put it there. This represents the professional identity formation with which law schools must wrestle as they help students move from law students to lawyers.

6. CLIENT MORALS, LAWYER MORALS, AND THE AUTOCRAT

In the family trust case, it may be that Ned Warren got what he wanted. He may have been like the client described by one of Louis Auchincloss's corporate-lawyer characters:

> Your client wants you to do something grasping and selfish. But quite within the law. You advise him that he can do it. So he does it and tells his victim, 'My lawyer made me!' You're satisfied and so is he.[30]

But Ned Warren told his brother Sam that he had doubts about the direction the representation was taking. Autocrats soothe such doubts, or ignore them. Ned may have been more like the personal injury client quoted by Douglas Rosenthal in his classic study of lawyer-client relations:

> [T]he lawyer is a reassuring presence who takes away your guilt feelings. He says, "Hey, this is the way the game is played; you take as much as you can get; it's what they expect; it's the way it's done." He takes upon his own shoulders the burden of your guilt—he's the professional.[31]

The client Rosenthal quoted assumed that the lawyer was bearing the burden of the client's guilt, but some lawyers have their own ways of dealing with moral responsibility. Professionalism and the adversary role invite us to maintain a distance from moral problems, a distance that tempts us away from moral responsibility. Rand Jack and Dana Crowley Jack did a series of interviews of lawyers which examined lawyers' views of morality and their work. Concerning one lawyer, they report:

> George Willis stresses his professionalism: "I'm a professional. I live and die by my reputation. I'm going to do a good job if I think you're an asshole, if I think you're a nice guy. I try and be as professional as possible and I try to have a thick skin." Here the term "professional" connotes a zealous loyalty of lawyer to client, and it is professionalism that allows this attorney's strong sense

[30] Louis Auchincloss, The Great World and Timothy Colt 75 (1956).

[31] Rosenthal, *supra* Chapter 1 note 16, at 1719, *quoted in* Simon, *The Ideology of Advocacy*, *supra* Chapter 1 note 10, at 117 n.198.

> of personal integrity. Professional commitment is juxtaposed with a thick skin, a barrier that limits the nature of attachment and separates emotion from action.[32]

Maybe this sort of detachment is necessary for lawyers who serve in a state system for resolving disputes through the adversarial process. If a lawyer thinks that the client is a terrible person and that the client is doing terrible things, the distance the lawyer maintains from the client frees the lawyer from responsibility for what the client does; the principle of nonaccountability frees the lawyer from responsibility for what the lawyer does. But, as Richard Wasserstrom says:

> [T]he lawyer as professional comes to inhabit a simplified universe which is strikingly amoral—which regards as morally irrelevant any number of factors which nonprofessional citizens might take to be important, if not decisive, in their everyday lives.[33]

The Autocrat comes to play an amoral role, at times even an immoral role. Lawyer and law student are invited to live a schizophrenic moral life, the role at the office strikingly different from who the lawyer is at home. Schizophrenia is bad enough; the greater danger is that the schizophrenia will be resolved in the wrong direction: The amorality of the advocate's role may come to dominate all of the lawyer's life.

Ned Warren may have gotten what he wanted in the family trust case, but maybe not. His letter to his brother seems to be sincere; it seems to be the letter of an "affectionate brother." It may be that neither Ned nor his lawyers, acting independently, would have filed the lawsuit that seems to have caused Sam's death. If Ned had had independent control over the representation, he might not have, in his words, "felt obliged" to make the accusations against his brother. If Ned's lawyer had been in Ned's shoes, he might not have accused his own brother of a breach of trust.

But it appears that no one took the moral implications of these "legal" decisions into consideration. Ned resolved the moral issue by deference to his lawyers and his lawyers resolved the moral issue by deference to their role as advocates for Ned's most selfish interests. This habit of dividing responsibility during legal representation leaves no place for morality: The lawyer pursues the client's *rights*. No one determines what would be the *right* thing to do. And no one seems concerned with being and becoming a better person.

---

[32] Rand Jack & Dana Crowley Jack, Moral Vision and Professional Decisions: The Changing Values of Women and Men Lawyers 104–05 (1989) (hereinafter "Moral Vision and Professional Decisions").

[33] Wasserstrom, *supra* Chapter 1 note 12, at 8.

CHAPTER 2

THE LAWYER AS HIRED GUN: CLIENT CONTROL AND CLIENT AUTONOMY

■ ■ ■

1. THE MALNOURISHED CHILD

The following is from Steven Wexler's account of his experiences as a lawyer for poor people. His practice was not what most people think of when they think of the practice of law; he suggests that the responsibility of a poor person's lawyer is "to strengthen existing organizations of poor people, and to help poor people start organizations where none exist."[1] Nevertheless, the role he advocates for lawyers *vis-a-vis* moral choices during representation is a familiar one.

* * *

> I went to talk to a local welfare rights group [WRO] in New Jersey. While I was there, two women who were not members of the group came in. One had been denied a welfare check to which she was entitled, the other had a severely malnourished child; both had heard that the local WRO might be able to help them. The group chairwoman, Mrs. Davis, suggested that the group go with the two women, first to the welfare office, then to the hospital.
>
> [At the welfare office, after] some scuffling, threats and negotiations, we had gotten an emergency check for both women. . . . I was able to support them with information and with my presence as a lawyer; I was fully committed to the action and never questioned the tactics or process they chose.
>
> After the welfare office victory, we went to the emergency room of the general hospital. The women went in and demanded that a doctor examine the baby. Flushed with the welfare office win, I went along with this tactic, although uneasily.
>
> After a little time had passed without a doctor appearing, the women walked into the hallways of the emergency ward, and, when that did not bring any action, they stopped a doctor and demanded that he examine the baby. The doctor, a small man who

[1] Steven Wexler, *Practicing Law for Poor People*, 79 YALE L.J. 1049, 1053–54 (1970).

spoke English only haltingly, explained that he could only treat for poisoning and convulsions. Malnutrition was not an emergency, and the baby would have to be brought back to the clinic on Monday morning. The women refused to accept this answer and surrounded the doctor (a somewhat comical picture: eight big women towering shoulder to shoulder around this small doctor), ordering him to examine the baby. He did so, and, though he could not be forced to prescribe anything for the baby, he was induced to write the mother a note indicating that she had been to the emergency room and should be seen first at the Monday clinic.

I was called on to do no more in the hospital than I had done in the welfare office. I remained physically with the women throughout the hospital action. I will not try to pick out the point at which I ceased to be emotionally in favor of the action; somewhere along the line my sympathy for people who have trouble speaking English, my faith in the doctors who had been so nice to a white boy in the suburbs, my feeling that hospital routine was more reasonable and justifiable than welfare office routine, my realization that there was "really nothing" that the doctor could do, my knowledge that we had no legal right to what we sought, and many other feelings of mine which the women did not share made me wish that I did not have to stay with them. Had I been able, I would have called the action off; had I realized what would happen at the hospital, I would have tried to dissuade the women from going there; I would never have thought of the relief that the women finally obtained. But forcing the doctor to write that note was a real victory for them. No lawyer has a right to deny them that victory by structuring the alternatives as he sees them or by denying the women the chance to choose their own way and use their lawyer to achieve their end. A lawyer must help them do their thing, or get out.[2]

* * *

The case of the malnourished child is a story of client control and attorney deference. Unlike the family estate story and the story of the Catholic Church (the lawyer as Autocrat), in which the lawyers controlled the decision-making guided by their perception of the financial interests of their clients, it is the client who controls direction in the malnourished child story. The client may or may not have considered the morality of the direction she takes and bids her lawyer to take.

Wexler says it was not the lawyer's business to consider the harm to the doctor or the other patients. The lawyer's job is to *empower* the client,

---

[2] *Id.* at 1064–65 (language updated, substituting "women" for "ladies").

not to question the client's morality. In Wexler's words, "A lawyer must help [clients] do their thing, or get out." In the common language of the public and many lawyers, the lawyer acts as a "Hired Gun."[3]

Under one moral justification for this model of legal representation, the lawyer's goal is the autonomy of the client. Autonomy is the ability to control one's life, the power to live independently. Its Greek components mean self-ruled. Wexler advocates client autonomy in this story about representing powerless people, but he and others also advocate autonomy for powerful clients.[4] Academic advocates of client autonomy come primarily from the fields of client counseling[5] and of legal ethics.[6] Those in client counseling often refer to legal counseling which has client autonomy as its aim as "client-centered" counseling.

Monroe Freedman, a professor of legal ethics, has said:

> One of the essential values of a just society is respect for the dignity of each member of that society. Essential to each individual's dignity is the free exercise of his autonomy. Toward that end, each person is entitled to know his rights with respect to society and other individuals, and to decide whether to seek fulfillment of those rights through the due processes of law. . . .
>
> [T]he attorney acts both professionally and morally in assisting clients to maximize their autonomy. . . . [T]he attorney acts unprofessionally and immorally by depriving clients of their autonomy, that is, by denying them information regarding their legal rights, by otherwise preempting their moral decisions, or by depriving them of the ability to carry out their lawful decisions.[7]

This focus on the ethics of autonomy is consistent with the ethics of the Enlightenment and the American political tradition that took a poisonous snake as its symbol under the motto, "Don't tread on me." It suggests that the highest good we can hope for our clients is that they be free. Under this view, the lawyer's moral task is to act in such a way as to

---

3 Wexler plays the role of Hired Gun as to moral issues that arise during representation—he leaves them to the client. In other respects he does not act as a Hired Gun—hired guns generally go to the highest bidder. Notably, the Hired Gun conception is not unique to American lawyers. One of the authors was visiting law schools in India a number of years ago where there were references to lawyers as "hired knife throwers."

4 Wexler, *supra* Chapter 2 note 1, at 1063; Charles Fried, *The Lawyer as Friend*, 85 YALE L.J. 1060 (1976); Stephen L. Pepper, *The Lawyer's Amoral Ethical Role: A Defense, A Problem, and Some Possibilities*, 1986 AM. B. FOUND. RES. J. 613, 616–19 (1986).

5 *See* David A. Binder *et al.*, Lawyers as Counselors: A Client-Centered Approach (2d ed. 2004); Robert M. Bastress & Joseph D. Harbaugh, Interviewing, Counseling, and Negotiating: Skills for Effective Representation (1990); David A. Binder & Susan C. Price, Legal Interviewing and Counseling: A Client-Centered Approach (1977).

6 *See* Monroe H. Freedman & Abbe Smith, Understanding Lawyers' Ethics (4th ed. 2010); Fried, *supra* Chapter 2 note 4; Pepper, *supra* Chapter 2 note 4.

7 Freedman & Smith, *supra* Chapter 2 note 6, at 62. *See also* Fried, *supra* Chapter 2 note 4, at 1073; Pepper, *supra* Chapter 2 note 4.

protect clients from the influence of others, so that clients will make their own moral rules, be their own rulers.[8]

2. CLIENT AUTONOMY AND HARM TO OTHERS

Of course, client autonomy has its costs, most obviously costs to other people, and to the relationships this ethic necessarily devalues. Client autonomy can harm people in the path the client takes. Edward Dauer and Arthur Leff put it this way:

> The client comes to a lawyer to be aided when he feels he is being treated, or wishes to treat someone else, not as a whole other person, but (at least in part) as a threat or hindrance to the client's satisfaction in life. The client has fallen, or wishes to thrust someone else, into the impersonal hands of a just and angry bureaucracy. When one desires help in those processes whereby and wherein people are treated as means and not as ends, then one comes to lawyers, to us.[9]

Dauer and Leff describe both the premises and likely consequences of Hired-Gun lawyering. We disagree with them in some respects. Clients more often come for help *in* their relationships than for help *from* their relationships. We think the problem is that many lawyers see their role as that described by Dauer and Leff; in the name of client autonomy, such lawyers "treat others as means and not as ends," whether that is the client's goal or not. Though he did not use the term "autonomy," the classic statement of the lawyer's duty to his client interests from the 19th century Scots barrister Lord Brougham similarly emphasizes attention to the interests of the client regardless of collateral damage.[10]

In the malnourished child case, a goal of client autonomy led to a small amount of harm to other people: The doctor was abused, his patients were delayed, and the clinic's patients lost their places in line on Monday morning. Because Wexler's clients had little power, their small claim to autonomy did little harm. But client autonomy for clients with great power (clients who produce dangerous products, have many employees, or have a great impact on the environment) can result in great harm to other people.

The "Hired Gun" lawyer we are describing is one responding to client control without accounting for concerns about others. Advocates of client

---

[8] Two of this book's authors, in the past, in advocating greater client control of legal representation *vis-à-vis* the attorney, have held up client autonomy as a goal. *See* Cochran, *Legal Representation and Client Control, supra* Chapter 1 note 16, at 830–33; Thomas L. Shaffer, On Being a Christian and a Lawyer 3–44 (1981). Though we continued to oppose lawyer dominance (*see* Chapters One and Three of the current volume), we came to believe, for all the reasons stated in this chapter, that the term "autonomy" carries with it too much additional baggage.

[9] Edward A. Dauer & Arthur A. Leff, *Correspondence: The Lawyer as Friend*, 86 YALE L.J. 573, 581 (1977).

[10] Brougham, *supra* Chapter 1 note 5.

autonomy and/or client-centered lawyering acknowledge space for the lawyer's morality or the lawyer's conscience, but place restraints on how the lawyer interjects conscience or morality in the name of client autonomy (though they generally provide some place for the lawyer's conscience).[11]

3. THE CLIENT-CENTERED COUNSELORS: LIMITS ON THE LAWYER'S CONSCIENCE DURING COUNSELING

Client-Centered Counseling Methods. Advocates of "client-centered" legal counseling include David Binder, Susan Price, Paul Bergman, Paul Tremblay, Robert Bastress, and Joseph Harbaugh. They draw their name, inspiration, and many of their methods from the "client-centered" theory of the late psychologist Carl Rogers.[12] Rogers believed in the fundamental goodness of humans, a belief shared by some of the client-centered legal counselors.[13] "In Rogerian thinking, each individual possesses an innate drive toward self-actualization (that is, toward autonomy, maturity, and self-fulfillment) and away from control by others."[14] Client-centered lawyers assist clients in fulfilling this drive toward self-actualization.

Client-centered legal counseling focuses on the desires of the client. Because client autonomy is of paramount importance, "decisions should be made on the basis of what choice is most likely to *provide clients with maximum satisfaction*."[15] The lawyer should not act in ways that would influence the client's choice. The lawyer should be "neutral"[16] and "nonjudgmental."[17] The lawyer should express empathy for the client's feelings, because, Bastress and Harbaugh say:

---

11 There is substantial disagreement among advocates of client autonomy about the place of the lawyer's conscience. Some suggest that the place for the lawyer's conscience is at the beginning—when the lawyer is deciding whom to represent (*see* Freedman and Smith, *supra* Chapter 2 note 6, at 52, 69–72); some suggest that the place of the lawyer's conscience is in the middle—that discussing moral issues with the client should be a part of the decision-making process (*see* Freedman and Smith, *supra* Chapter 2 note 6, at 54; Fried, *supra* Chapter 2 note 4, at 1088; Pepper, *supra* Chapter 2 note 4, at 632); and some suggest that the place of the lawyer's conscience is at the end—that lawyers should challenge client decisions that they believe to be wrong (*see* Binder *et al.*, *supra* Chapter 2 note 5, at 282, 292–95; Bastress & Harbaugh, *supra* Chapter 2 note 5, at 334–35), and withdraw if clients do not pursue a different course (*see id.*). *See also infra* text accompanying notes 29 to 40.

12 *See, e.g.*, Bastress & Harbaugh, *supra* Chapter 2 note 5, at 57.

13 *Id.* at 27 and 57. For a description of Rogers's theory of psychology, *see id.* at 26–32. For a criticism of Rogers's focus on self-actualization and its impact on moral responsibility, *see* William H. Simon, *Homo Psychologicus: Notes on a New Legal Formalism*, 32 STAN. L. REV. 487, 511–16 (1980).

14 Bastress & Harbaugh, *supra* Chapter 2 note 5, at 28.

15 Binder *et al.*, *supra* Chapter 2 note 5, at 272 (original emphasis). *See also* Bastress & Harbaugh, *supra* Chapter 2 note 5, at 256.

16 Binder & Price, *supra* Chapter 2 note 5, at 166; Binder *et al.*, *supra* Chapter 2 note 5, at 300.

17 Bastress & Harbaugh, *supra* Chapter 2 note 5, at 57.

> You communicate respect through . . . accurate empathy; your understanding of the client's feelings and experiences necessarily implies that the client has acted, or reacted, in a way that is natural and appropriate. That is, the client's feelings and experiences are "understandable."[18]

However, as Stephen Ellman has noted, "It is hard to escape the conclusion that what is 'natural and appropriate,' and thus 'understandable,' is also 'right.' "[19]

When a decision is to be made in legal representation, client-centered advocates suggest that the lawyer and client list on a sheet of paper all the alternative courses of action and the potential consequences to the client of each.[20] Under the Bastress and Harbaugh model, the consequences are labeled "consequences for client." The lawyer asks probing questions that will help lawyer and client to more fully understand the consequences for the client. The client then decides among the alternatives.

Bastress and Harbaugh suggest that prior to the counseling session, the lawyer prepare a counseling plan. In their book, the hypothetical case that introduces and illustrates their method involves Ralph Kratzer, a long-time friend and neighbor of the client. Kratzer has opened a bar next door to the client which may violate a zoning ordinance. Bastress and Harbaugh set up a portion of the counseling plan as follows:

Alternative	Consequences for Client	Probing subjects
File Civil Action	Strain on relationship with Kratzer	How important to the client is his friendship with Kratzer?[21]

The plan lists several other consequences for the client of filing a civil action, including "time and effort required," "money to pay for fees and expenses," and "exposure to deposition and trial examination." There is no mention of the effect of the action on Kratzer. The consequences to Kratzer of the client's filing suit are considered solely in light of the effect that they will have on the client; Kratzer has no independent moral significance. The "plan" suggests that if Kratzer were not a friend or if the client's friendship with Kratzer were not seen by the client as important, Kratzer would not be worthy of consideration.

---

[18] Bastress & Harbaugh, *supra* Chapter 2 note 5, at 130, *quoted in* Stephen Ellman, *Empathy and Approval*, 43 HASTINGS L.J. 991, 993 (1992).

[19] Ellman, *Empathy and Approval*, *supra* Chapter 2 note 18, at 993.

[20] Binder & Price, *supra* Chapter 2 note 5, at 184; Bastress & Harbaugh, *supra* Chapter 2 note 5, at 246–49; Binder *et al.*, *supra* Chapter 2 note 5, at 300.

[21] Bastress & Harbaugh, *supra* Chapter 2 note 5, at 246.

Binder and Price also view moral problems during the counseling process in terms of consequences to the client.[22] They give the example of a client who is charged with a criminal offense. The client is considering a plea bargain that would require her to admit that the police had probable cause for the client's arrest. The client objects, "I would be admitting something I don't believe." The lawyer responds, "I can tell that would really bother you. Do you think it would bother you for a long time?"[23] Here, Stephen Ellman suggests, the lawyer translates "the client's desire to act in a morally correct and socially responsible way [telling the truth] into a psychological need to avoid guilt."[24]

As noted previously, the client-centered legal counselors are influenced by the theories of psychologist Carl Rogers, but there may be dangers in seeing clients as patients. It may be that the client-centered counselors have adopted techniques from a field of psychotherapy that are not appropriate for legal clients. Psychotherapists often treat psychological difficulties by freeing patients from damaging relationships of overdependence. The client-centered counselors (and some popular psychologists) have taken a jump from what may be a valuable insight in treating psychological difficulties to the assumption that everyone should be freed from the influence of other people. But, as philosopher Mary Midgley writes, counseling people to focus on their own interests

> is understandable as a piece of crisis-management for particular cases—for abnormal dependence, abnormal submissiveness and conformity. Or again, it can be seen as a half-truth of value for all of us. Self-respect, self-understanding, and indeed self-love, are necessary parts of serious living; they are not guilty excesses; we vitally need them. . . .
>
> But it is surely alarming to preach this gospel as normal and comprehensive advice for most people.[25]

The client-centered counselors argue that their methods are neutral, but we think their methods influence clients to make self-serving choices.

---

[22] Binder and Price, in their 1977 book, suggest that lawyers and clients consider "social consequences," but in all the examples they give of lawyers and clients considering "social consequences," the focus is on the consequences to the client. *See, e.g.*, Binder & Price, *supra* Chapter 2 note 5, at 139, 145, 151.

In the more recent (2004) book from Binder, Bergman, Price, and Tremblay, the authors note that if clients "fail to recognize that one or more of their possible alternatives may have a substantial positive or negative impact on third parties or society in general . . . you may well want to call such possibilities to their attention." Binder *et al.*, *supra* Chapter 2 note 5, at 308. At the conclusion of the counseling process, they suggest, the lawyer might question the decision of the client on moral grounds, under the procedure discussed *infra* at text accompanying notes 31–32.

[23] Binder & Price, *supra* Chapter 2 note 5, at 178. Binder and Price indicate approval of the lawyer's response. *Id.* at 182.

[24] Stephen Ellman, *Lawyers and Clients*, 34 UCLA L. REV. 717, 750 (1987) (hereinafter "*Lawyers and Clients*").

[25] Mary Midgley, Can't We Make Moral Judgements? 121 (1991).

The lawyer and client consider alternatives in light of "consequences for the client," not consequences for others. The client might independently raise the interests of others, but the lawyer seems to diminish this concern. The client is likely to look to the lawyer to take the lead in the lawyer-client relationship, and if the lawyer identifies some considerations that are important (consequences to the client) and fails to identify other considerations (consequences to others), the client is likely to assume that consequences to others are not relevant in the law office, even though they might actually be meaningful to the client.[26] As a result, during decision-making under client-centered counseling, the lawyer likely will act in a manner similar to the Autocrat discussed in the previous chapter—steering the client toward a narrow, selfish goal.

The client-centered counselors' claim of neutrality fails to recognize that the lawyer-client relationship is a moral relationship, one in which the parties influence one another for good or for ill. The product of their moral conversation (moral whether or not they think of it that way) is the product of mutuality: poor, unrecognized, hampered mutuality, perhaps, but mutuality nonetheless. Louis Auchincloss's corporate official said, "My lawyer made me do it," as Wexler may say, "My client made me do it," but those are evasions of the fact that both lawyer and client are present and involved in the decision-making; the course taken belongs to both of them. As the existentialist philosophers say, "What is not possible is not to choose."

People involved in intense relationships—and many lawyer-client relationships are intense—change. They employ old moral habits—old virtues and vices. They strengthen these habits, or weaken them, or take on new ones. They *become* better people or worse people. Part of the question here—perhaps the largest part—for the lawyer might be, "What is this other person becoming because of me, and what am I becoming because of this other person?" We fear that client-centered counseling tends toward bad moral formation, leaving clients (and lawyers) more focused on their own interests, and less concerned with the interests of others, than they were when they came into the relationship.[27] Even for clients who want to be in control of making decisions, who want to assert their autonomy, the framework provided by the Hired Gun may be poorly aligned with the client's interests if the client wants to engage in moral conversations or discuss how the client's decision might impact others. As noted above, the counseling design for the Hired Gun is one that ignores or diminishes any concern for others because client autonomy is understood to be self-focused rather than other-directed. Thus, by steering away from conversations about morality or conscience or impacts on others, Hired Gun

---

[26] *See* Ellman, *Lawyers and Clients*, *supra* Chapter 2 note 24, at 749.

[27] Client-centered counselors discourage lawyers from offering advice to clients, unless clients request it. *See, e.g.*, Binder *et al.*, *supra* Chapter 2 note 5, at 289–92, 368–70.

lawyers may be failing to adequately serve the interests of clients who would like to integrate moral concerns into their decision-making but may need help in doing so.

Client-Centered Counseling and Moral Direction. Bastress and Harbaugh recognize the danger that client-centered counseling will leave lawyers as Hired Guns:

> [We have] advocated a model of the lawyer-client relationship that requires you to be empathetic, nonjudgmental, and solicitous of client decision-making. This model, however, if stretched to an apparently logical extreme, could render you totally amoral in your professional relations with clients, bound only by your client's desires and the limits of the law.[28]

The client-centered counselors suggest that the lawyer's conscience might legitimately come into play when the client makes a decision which the lawyer believes is morally wrong.[29]

Following those chapters of their book that outline the client-centered decision-making process, Bastress and Harbaugh include an excerpt from an article by Bastress, which suggests the following after the client makes a choice:

> The lawyer should then independently assess the case to determine if she has any moral or social objections, both in terms of the consequences to the immediate parties and of the effects on broader policy implications. If so, then she should . . . fully discuss the issue with the client. The client may satisfy the lawyer's reservations and the representation can then continue. If, however, the client cannot meet the lawyer's objections, then the lawyer should explore possible alternatives with the client. If that fails, then the lawyer should again exercise her independent judgment and, if the concern persists and is serious, should refuse to proceed with the case. The judgment should be based on the lawyer's personal sense of right and justice. . . .[30]

Binder, Bergman, Price, and Tremblay also allow lawyers to raise moral concerns. "[C]lient-centeredness need not cause you to wholly abandon your moral commitments. When clients opt for courses of action that you believe are morally repugnant (though lawful), self-respect for your own autonomy may make it appropriate for you to ask them to reconsider their decisions."[31]

---

[28] Bastress & Harbaugh, *supra* Chapter 2 note 5, at 321.

[29] *Id.* at 334–35; Binder *et al.*, *supra* Chapter 2 note 5 at 293–95. Binder and Price's earlier counseling book provides no place for moral counsel. *See* Binder & Price, *supra* Chapter 2 note 5.

[30] Bastress & Harbaugh, *supra* Chapter 2 note 5, at 334–35.

[31] Binder *et al.*, *supra* Chapter 2 note 5, at 293.

The place client-centered counselors give for the exercise of the lawyer's conscience is important in its recognition that lawyers have consciences and that in some circumstances lawyers should exercise conscientious objection. They propose a sort of moral discourse, however, that we believe presents problems.

First, client-centered counselors' moral discourse comes into play only when the lawyer feels that the client wants to do something that is "morally repugnant."[32] Morality (in and out of the law office) is not generally a matter of choosing whether to do something that is morally repugnant; more often it is a choice between something that is better and something that is worse. It may not be often that the client will make a choice that the lawyer feels is "morally repugnant," but clients constantly are faced with issues that have moral implications. We feel that those moral implications should be considered during the decision-making process.

For example, in the case discussed from Bastress and Harbaugh in which the client is considering suing Kratzer, his "long time friend and neighbor," over a zoning matter, a lawyer is unlikely to conclude that the decision to sue Kratzer is *immoral*—Kratzer did open a bar next to the client's house. But suing Kratzer may not be the best thing to do, and determining the best thing to do should include thinking about Kratzer's interests, whether or not the lawyer would ultimately consider the decision to sue Kratzer to be morally wrong. Kratzer's interest is a moral consideration, but not one in which the lawyer's hesitation is best expressed as an ultimate judgment. The lawyer's contribution to the conversation might be more like a concern or a question—something a friend would say to a friend. Most of our ordinary moral impulses are like that—morals being, then, the subject of a moral discussion.

There is an unjustified finality in the lawyer's moral impulse as it is described by the client-centered counselors. There is too much lonely independence in it. It is too little like the ordinary conversations we have with family, friends, neighbors, and associates about what to do. In ordinary conversation we propose, try out, suggest, and listen. We rarely issue moral pronouncements arrived at "independently" and outside of ordinary, tentative, mutual conversation. We are not ordinarily conscientious objectors in our relationships with other people.

Second, we think that the method of moral discourse suggested by the client-centered counselors is likely to be ineffective. The client is likely to feel a sense of betrayal after the lawyer leads the client to consider a decision in terms of narrow client interest and then challenges the client's decision. The client may well feel that the lawyer was involved in making the decision and has in some significant way become committed to it. In addition, when clients have decided what to do following a counseling

[32] *Id.*

session, it is unlikely they will admit that they were wrong. Once they make a decision, clients are likely to grow in their commitment to it. Finally, lawyers are likely to recognize the futility of such a challenge and not even make the effort. After lawyers encourage the client to see things from the client's perspective and the client makes a decision, it will be difficult for lawyers to shift gears and reverse the direction of the counseling. Morals at that point seem too much like an intrusion on "legal business."

4. MONROE FREEDMAN: LIMITS ON THE LAWYER'S CONSCIENCE AFTER THE CLIENT'S DECISION

Monroe Freedman appears to take a position that is the opposite of that of the client-centered counselors on the proper place of client autonomy and lawyer conscience.[33] Freedman argues, as we do, for the exercise of moral influence during the counseling process. In his words, lawyers should counsel their clients "regarding . . . moral responsibilities as the lawyer perceives them."[34] But Freedman also argues that if the client makes a choice which the lawyer believes is immoral but legal, the lawyer should assist the client.[35]

Freedman illustrates both parts of this point—the moral counsel part, and the moral deference part—with examples from his own practice. In one case, his client, a landlord, wanted Freedman to evict a widow and her children. Freedman said, "If you want to evict her, I will. But why don't you give the matter some thought." The client decided not to evict her. In the other case, the other side had made a damaging error in a contract. Freedman said: "We can clobber them with it," and the client cheered. Then Freedman said: "The other choice is to call them up and point out the error. That way, you are the good guy, and maybe we can put our future relationship with them on a higher plane by setting the example." The client took the latter course.[36]

---

[33] Professor Freedman adopted the term "client-centered" to describe his autonomy-grounded theory of legal ethics, though, as the text argues, his model differs significantly from that of the client-centered counselors. *See* the exchange between Professors Freedman and Cochran at Robert F. Cochran, Jr., *Enlightenment Liberalism, Lawyers, and the Future of Lawyer-Client Relations*, 33 CAMPBELL L. REV. 685 (2011); Monroe H. Freedman, *Client-Centered Lawyering—What It Isn't*, 40 HOFSTRA L. REV. 349 (2012); and Robert F. Cochran, Jr., *Which Client-Centered Counselors?: A Reply to Professor Freedman*, 40 HOFSTRA L. REV. 355–66 (2012) (hereinafter "*Which Client-Centered Counselors?*".

[34] Monroe H. Freedman, *Personal Responsibility in a Professional System*, 27 CATH. U. L. REV. 191 (1978).

[35] Charles Fried and Stephen Pepper appear to also advocate both moral counsel and continued representation despite a lawyer's moral objections to client decisions. *See* Fried, *supra* Chapter 2 note 4, at 1088, 1089; Pepper, *supra* Chapter 2 note 4, at 632–635.

[36] Letter from Monroe H. Freedman to Thomas L. Shaffer (Aug. 22, 1986).

But in both cases Freedman said he would do what the client wanted, even if the client chose to be ruthless. Freedman says to clients, I will tell you what I think you should do, but if you decide to do something else—even something I regard as immoral—I will help you do it.

Freedman argues that if lawyers refuse to help clients pursue their lawful objectives, lawyers thereby deprive clients of their "rights."[37] We agree with William Simon that Freedman's argument

> conflates an opportunity to obtain an advantage from a legal institution with a right. . . . To invoke the client's right in a normative sense—to hold that clients have an ethical claim to anything that the courts can be made to yield—presupposes a view of the legal system that few lawyers take seriously. . . .[38]

We think lawyers should remain open to the moral influences of their clients, but surely they should not surrender their own moral responsibility in the process. That surrender weakens the effects of the lawyer's good character that the client may need and may have come to get. The issue is not moral counsel; we agree with Freedman on that. The question is: What makes moral counsel coherent? Moral counsel comes from our oldest ethical traditions. It is what Thomas Aquinas called fraternal correction,[39] what Karl Barth called conditional advice.[40] Effective, valuable moral advice is most likely to come from a whole, integrated, human person, a person who is consistent and whose hope is that the client will be and become a better person.

We will argue in Chapter Four for a model in which lawyers counsel their clients as they would counsel good friends. Lawyers should be concerned that clients be and become better people, just as friends are concerned that one another be good. Friends are faithful to one another; they hesitate to part company, and we think lawyers should be that way with their clients. Nevertheless, parting may come. In our view, a lawyer should withdraw from representation when the client wants her to do something the lawyer believes to be morally wrong.[41]

Conditional advice—moral advice—fraternal correction—is of little value unless such integrity is mutually understood. Moral advice depends

---

[37] *See supra* text at Chapter 2 note 7, *quoting* Freedman and Smith. Charles Fried makes the same argument. *See* Fried, *supra* Chapter 2 note 4, at 1073.

[38] William H. Simon, *Ethical Discretion in Lawyering*, 101 HARV. L. REV. 1083, 1123 (1988) (hereinafter "*Ethical Discretion*"); *see also* Gerald J. Postema, *Moral Responsibility in Professional Ethics*, 55 N.Y.U. L. REV. 63, 85–86 (1980) (making a similar argument in response to Charles Fried).

[39] *See* Thomas Aquinas, Summa Theologica II, Q 33, 1333–41 (Fathers of the English Dominican Province trans., 1947).

[40] *See* Karl Barth, The Epistle to the Romans (Hoskyns trans., 6th ed. 1968).

[41] *See* infra Chapter 4, Section 11. For further discussion of moral responsibility, Monroe Freedman, and the Client-Centered counselors, see Cochran, *Which Client-Centered Counselors?*, *supra* Chapter 2 note 33, at 355–66.

on character and on the perception, in the person seeking the advice, that the advisor is a person of character. We suspect Monroe Freedman's clients listened to him because he was a person of character. That is why they changed their minds and followed his advice. That is likely to be what influenced them, not his saying that he would do for them whatever they wanted done.

5. THE MYTH OF AUTONOMY AND THE REALITY OF INFLUENCE

Proponents of client autonomy argue that clients should be free from the influence of the attorney and free from the influence of others. We agree with proponents of client autonomy that lawyers should not dictate the course of representation. Lawyers should help clients have control over their lives because the law at its best serves the dignity of persons—not because clients are or should be self-ruling.

Though we think lawyers should not dominate the relationship, it is unrealistic to suggest that lawyers can, and unwise to suggest that they should, avoid influencing their clients. It is incorrect to suggest that clients—to suggest that any of us—could or *should* exist in the lonely privacy the ethics of autonomy assumes. We are all dependent on others. Clients—just as a matter of anthropology—are not independent. As we illustrated above, even the theory of client counseling which claims to be neutral is not; client-centered lawyers *lead* clients to focus on their own interests, rather than the interests of others. In this respect the model violates its own claim to respect client autonomy. It discourages what may be a client's desire to make moral choices. It is important that lawyers recognize the influence they have, and which clients seek, so that lawyers can use influence wisely. Pretending that lawyers can avoid influence merely enables lawyers to avoid taking responsibility for the influence they have.

Our great story-tellers, Austen, Eliot, Tolstoy, Chekhov, Snow, Melville, Faulkner, Tolkien, and Tyler, say that we want to be, and we want others to be, brave, generous, reverent, cheerful, and honest. We want to have those virtues, and to learn how to practice them, as we live and work with other people. As Socrates said, we want to *be good*, and we want others, and especially those closest to us, to be good. We don't want our trusted advisors to be neutral; we want them to be *wise*. The logic of our lives together—something frequently displayed in our lawyer-hero stories, from *To Kill a Mockingbird* to *Law and Order*—is that we do not lose our freedom when we influence and are influenced. We are radically connected to one another. The human person comes to *be* in relationships—in families, congregations, communities, friendships, and associations. When you describe our lives carefully, you describe lives of moral influence.

6. THE LAWYER AS ADVOCATE: THE GOOD-OF-THE-CLIENT ARGUMENT

In Chapter One, we considered the argument that the lawyer's adversary role is for the good of society, the argument that the adversarial system will yield a just result. The good-of-the-client argument for the adversary system is somewhat more modest. It is that, irrespective of harm to others, aggressive advocacy is for the good of the client. Lawyers who focus on client autonomy argue that they cannot be responsible to anyone except their clients.

"Autonomy" carries with it the view of each person as a bundle of rights that will enable him or her to become more and more independent of others. But complete independence from others is usually not in the client's interest, even if it were possible. If a client comes to talk with a lawyer about marital difficulties, and if client autonomy is the lawyer's goal, does the goal of the representation automatically become divorce? Mutual dependence is one of the greatest joys of marriage, but can a person subject to such dependence be autonomous? Proponents of client autonomy might suggest that the goal here is for the client to determine whether dependence is in his or her interest, and we would agree. But if the lawyer goes into the representation assuming that client autonomy is the goal, we fear that the lawyer is likely to lead the client toward separation.

Holding up autonomy as the central goal of legal representation suggests that dependence is an evil, that it diminishes a person. Admittedly, a person can become over-dependent, but surely, ordinary dependence is a good thing. When we hear people speak of autonomy as if it were the greatest good, we are reminded of C.S. Lewis's picture of hell: Autonomous people on the outskirts of a city who continually move further and further away from one another.[42] That does not strike us as the good of society, nor as a good thing for people.

7. MORAL RESPONSIBILITY, HIRED GUNS, AND PROSTITUTES

Legal representation that focuses on the autonomy of the client can be bad for third parties and bad for clients, but it can also be bad for lawyers. This can present a different type of alignment problem for lawyers and clients. It imposes limits on the lawyer's conscience. Lawyers who are devoted to client autonomy operate on a curious sort of vicarious morality. They act for another, pursue the ends of another. They invite moral conflict as they do things for clients that they believe are wrong.

[42] C.S. Lewis, The Great Divorce 18–19 (1946).

Lawyers who pursue client autonomy may claim that they are free from moral responsibility. As Deborah Rhode has said:

> Those who refuse to pass judgment on a client generally seem to assume that such neutrality is value-free. But individuals cannot market their loyalty, avert their eyes to the consequences, and pretend they have not made a normative decision. To decline to take a moral stance is in itself a moral stance and requires justification as such. Thus the critical question is not by what right do lawyers impose their views, but by what right do they evade the responsibility of all individuals to evaluate the normative implications of their acts? Alternatively, by what right do clients circumscribe counsels' ethical duty?[43]

Hired Gun lawyers, like Autocrat lawyers, play a role that controls their moral choices. There are dangers in role-playing, even if role-playing serves the system and the client. One of the dangers for lawyers who live a divided life is that lawyerly practices can bleed over into other areas of life. The advocate role may come to dominate all of the lawyer's life if the lawyer is not conscious of its dangers and it is not properly contained. Morality is a skill like other skills; it is something we learn by doing. As we address problems morally, we develop the capacity to deal morally with other problems. If moral sensitivity has no place in lawyers' daily lives, they run the risk that their moral sensitivity will atrophy.[44] A lawyer who is deceptive or aggressive toward opposing parties, opposing lawyers, or juries today is likely to be deceptive to clients, judges, partners, neighbors, family, and friends tomorrow. At a minimum, lawyers need to be aware of these risks and resist them.

The ethic of vicarious conscience, of role, is morally schizoid; at best, it divides people up, and at worst it gives them excuses for immoral behavior. "Either the moral personality is entirely fragmented or compartmentalized, or it is shrunk to fit the moral universe defined by the role."[45]

Many lawyers feel uncomfortable when the Hired Gun role requires them to do something on behalf of the client that they believe is wrong. Many women lawyers that Rand Jack and Dana Crowley Jack interviewed used a vivid metaphor for expressing this moral pain:

> Words that denote involuntary or commercial sex reveal how deeply the intimate self of a lawyer at times feels violated by role requirements. Janice Orens: "It's like being forced into a sex relationship you didn't anticipate. It's a screw job. It feels horrible to do something that you wouldn't do normally." Diana

---

43 Deborah L. Rhode, *Ethical Perspectives on Legal Practice*, 37 STAN. L. REV. 589, 623 (1985).

44 Postema, *supra* Chapter 2 note 38, at 79.

45 *Id.* at 81.

> Cartwright: "I have to contradict myself depending on what role I'm taking . . . It's sort of professional prostitution."[46]

There may be a basis for the sense of guilt that these lawyers express. At least the burden of proof should be on those who argue that lawyers should do something they believe is immoral.

[46] Jack & Jack, Moral Vision and Professional Decisions, *supra* Chapter 1 note 32, at 112; *see also* Cramton, *supra* Chapter 1 note 6, 247, 259–60.

CHAPTER 3

THE LAWYER AS GURU: LAWYER CONTROL AND CLIENT RECTITUDE

■ ■ ■

1. THE SEGREGATED FACTORIES

The following is the account by one of your authors, Tom Shaffer, of his introduction to the practice of law:

* * *

The first large job I had involved President Kennedy's executive order on equal employment opportunity. This (1961 and 1962) was before the days of modern federal civil rights legislation. There was no clear federal law prohibiting racial discrimination in employment, and our clients in several parts of the country maintained racially segregated factories. One of our best clients had factories that were segregated according to the procedures of the Old South—separate jobs, separate areas of work, separate rest rooms, separate cafeterias. That corporate client, through its secretary, wanted to know what President Kennedy's order would require of it. The client was one we gave especially good service to. It had become large enough to have set up its own internal legal department, but had not taken that step, and we, of course, did not want it to take that step. We acted, and were happy to act, as if we were the internal legal department, and we thought we did a better job than an "in-house" set of lawyers could have done. There was folklore in the firm that said one of our senior partners had got up from a treatment table in the hospital to take a phone call involving this client's business. . . .

President Kennedy's executive order required that government contractors integrate their work forces. It bore most directly on contractors that sold to the federal government. Our client had virtually no business with the federal government. If the executive order was inconvenient for it, it could drop the government business without serious harm. But the order also had provisions covering second and third and fourth tier government contractors—companies that sold to companies that sold to the government, and so on. The regulations grew weaker as the chain grew longer. Our client, which did business mostly in the third or fourth link of the chain, was required to do little integrating, and even then it was unlikely that the regulations would be enforced on a company that was so peripheral to the federal enterprise. It was unlikely, really, that President Kennedy and his advisors had companies like our client in mind. The "bottom line," as we came later to call terse conclusions in business, was that our client had to do nothing.

I reported this in elaborate detail to the partner I worked under [a conservative, Goldwater Republican]. He heard me out, asked some questions, and said he understood. He said he would call the corporate secretary of our client, who had referred the question to us, and asked me to stay in his office while he did that—on a "squawk box" telephone that would allow me to join in the conversation from across the partner's desk. I sat there while the partner and the secretary and I worked through my arcane analysis, and they came to understand that the law was not a threat to our client's segregated factories.

The secretary said, at the end of all this, "Well, what do you think we ought to do?" My senior in the practice of law said, "Oh, I don't think there's much doubt about what you ought to do; I think you ought to integrate those factories." The secretary said, "All right," and hung up his telephone. I did some other work for this client, at its factories in the South, about a year later. They were well into the integration of the factories, and well into the social, political, and business turmoil that accompanied such changes in 1962.[1]

* * *

This seems to be a story of a client whose representative deferred to the lawyer, and of a lawyer who was quite willing to tell the client what good morals require. Here, as in the family trust story (the lawyer as Autocrat), it appears that the lawyer controls the choice and the client defers to the lawyer. But, whereas the lawyer in the family trust story made the choice based on the client's financial interests, here the elder lawyer apparently made the choice based on what he perceived to be the right moral direction. Maybe the lawyer was concerned with more than the client. Maybe he was concerned with the impact of what the client did on others. Maybe the lawyer's concern was that the client do the right thing.

The research Tom Shaffer did was about the law and what the law said the client "had to do" or "didn't have to do." Shaffer concluded that the law didn't require the client to do anything. This was a response to an implicit

---

1 Thomas L. Shaffer, Faith and the Professions 133–34 (1987).

question from the client regarding what the client "can do" that is consistent with the law. The client's inquiry of the partner, however, was a normative question. What should the client do? The partner was prepared to and comfortable answering this "should" question and directing the client in a moral direction.

The elder lawyer in this story is different in two respects from lawyers who place client autonomy as the central goal of the relationship. First, the moral responsibilities of the client to others are a concern in the lawyer-client relationship; second, the client appears to play a limited role in determining what those moral responsibilities are.

We refer to the lawyer who makes moral choices for clients as "Guru," because that is what gurus do: they tell their followers what to do.[2] As we will show, there is a long tradition in the United States of lawyers making decisions for clients based on the common good. The founders of American legal ethics, David Hoffman and George Sharswood,[3] are 19th century examples. More recent proponents of the lawyer as Guru include William Simon,[4] Deborah Rhode,[5] and David Luban.[6]

2. TRADITIONAL AMERICAN LAWYERS

The apparent pattern of moral advice in the segregated factories story is that of the traditional American lawyer. The traditional American lawyer had a stubborn, domineering moral orientation. The morals of the traditional lawyer were described and codified in the earliest American statements of lawyer morality—what David Hoffman (1784–1854), the grandfather of legal ethics among English-speaking lawyers, called "deportment." The traditional lawyer's influence remains in some law firms and small-town legal communities and continues to be passed on to apprentice lawyers.

Traditional lawyers are familiar from popular American lawyer stories. An example is Atticus Finch, of *To Kill a Mockingbird*.[7] Finch's Black client, Tom Robinson, was falsely accused of raping a White woman,

---

[2] Within the Hindu faith, the guru is far more directive than leaders within most Western religious traditions. This direction extends to the details of religious, moral, business and family matters. *See* Raymond B. Williams, *The Guru as Pastoral Counselor*, 40 J. OF PASTORAL CARE 331 (1986). "[The Guru's] Disciple must keep his defenses lowered and confidently yield to the Master." Dima S. Oueini, *The Guru and His Disciple*, 45 THE UNESCO COURIER 16 (Sept. 1992).

[3] *See infra* text accompanying notes 9, 16 and 17.

[4] Simon finds support for his position in the writings of David Hoffman and George Sharswood. *See* William H. Simon, The Practice of Justice: A Theory of Lawyers' Ethics 63–64 (1998) (hereinafter "The Practice of Justice").

[5] Deborah L. Rhode, In the Interests of Justice: Reforming the Legal Profession 58 (2000) (hereinafter "In the Interests of Justice").

[6] David Luban, *The Adversary System Excuse*, *in* The Good Lawyer: Lawyers' Roles and Lawyers' Ethics 118 (David Luban ed., 1984) (hereinafter "*The Adversary System Excuse*").

[7] *See* Harper Lee, To Kill a Mockingbird (1960).

Mayella Ewell. Atticus told his client that he *had to* come into court and tell the truth about his encounter with Mayella.

Note that Finch's moral imperative overrode Tom Robinson's autonomy. Finch did not discuss this moral concern with Robinson and frame a decision for Robinson to make about whether to testify.[8] Rather, Finch, as Guru, made the moral decision for Robinson through Finch's moral lens. Robinson deferred to Finch's judgment at great risk; he lost both his case and his life.

The advice was moral advice; it came from Finch's intense moral attachment to truthfulness and from what may have been a naive hope that his fellow citizens on the jury (or at least the appellate judges who reviewed them) would hear the truth, recognize the truth, and act according to the truth. And Finch did not shrink from responsibility both for the trial tactic he advised and the consequences of the tactic. What he advised was martyrdom, and he might well have claimed, as anyone who advises martyrdom, from Antigone to Jesus to the military officer who sends his troops into certain but noble death, that the advice was morally sound.

3. REJECTION OF ROLE: A UNIFIED ETHIC

In the first two chapters of this book, we talked about lawyers who played roles. Though they might have exercised strong moral values in their personal lives, in their professional lives they played the role of Autocrat or Hired Gun for the client. Perhaps the lawyer in the segregated factories case avoided the problem of vicarious morality by refusing to exercise role morality. He did not ascertain, or seek to ascertain, or to guess at, the narrow interest of his client (even though the young lawyer in the case thought that was the agenda and assembled his research to support a narrow interest).

Lawyers who control moral choices in representation need not follow a separate morality in professional life. As Atticus Finch put it, he had to be the same person in town and at home. He did not allow himself to defer to a "role" when he thought of the morals of being an advocate. He was not an agent for a principal in the moral life; he took moral responsibility for what he did and for what his clients did with his advice. Such lawyer principles of professional behavior are built upon, consistent with, and extensions of the behavior such lawyers learn in their families, neighborhoods, towns, and religious congregations.

---

[8] Notably, subsequent to the publication of To Kill a Mockingbird, the ABA promulgated the Model Rules of Professional Conduct. Finch's conduct in directing Robinson to testify would have been in violation of Rule 1.2a which provides that in criminal matters, defense clients always have the final say on pleas, plea agreements, jury trial waiver, and whether the client testifies. MODEL RULES OF PRO. CONDUCT r. 1.2a (Am. Bar Ass'n 2023).

4. TAKING RESPONSIBILITY

One of the consistent characteristics of the traditional lawyers in our American stories is that they take responsibility for everything that comes their way. Traditional lawyers make moral choices because they consider that they have responsibility for their clients and for the community. Their responsibility for their clients and for society is to see that they do the right thing. We find this acceptance of responsibility in the early lawyer codes. Professional responsibility (not a term they used) meant responsibility for justice. David Hoffman said that lawyers should not advocate a legal position unless they believe that the position is good for the country. "[S]hould the principle . . . be wholly at variance with sound law," he said, "it would be dishonorable folly in me to endeavor to incorporate it into the jurisprudence of the country."[9]

We find this sense of responsibility more recently in William Simon, Deborah Rhode, and David Luban. In Simon's book, *The Practice of Justice: A Theory of Lawyers' Ethics,* he argues: "Lawyers should take those actions that, considering the relevant circumstances of the particular case, seem likely to promote justice."[10] Simon suggests that lawyers determine what is just in the way judges and public prosecutors do.[11] Simon's analogies between the lawyer and the judge and prosecutor suggest (as Hoffman did) a lack of responsibility in the client. Clients are meant to defer to the consciences of their lawyers.

In her book *In the Interests of Justice* Deborah Rhode argues that "[l]awyers can, and should, act on the basis of their own principled convictions, even when they recognize that others could in good faith hold different views."[12] David Luban advocates a "moral activist" lawyer, arguing in his book *The Good Lawyer* that "when professional and moral

---

[9] "Resolutions on Professional Deportment," No. XIV, *in* I Hoffman, a Course of Legal Study (2d ed. 1836), *quoted in* Shaffer, Faith and the Professions, *supra* Chapter 3 note 1, at 64.

[10] Simon, The Practice of Justice, *supra* Chapter 3 note 4, at 138. Simon suggests that "justice" is synonymous with "legal merit" and "connotes the basic values of the legal system." *Id.* This chapter will discuss Simon's suggestion that the lawyer, rather than the client, should make the moral choices during legal representation. Chapter Six, Section One, will discuss Simon's suggestion that legal values should be the source of moral values during legal representation.

[11] *Id.* at 10–11, 139. The duty of the public prosecutor is "to seek justice, not merely to convict." *Id.* at 10, *quoting* MODEL CODE OF PRO. RESP. EC 7–13 (AM. BAR ASS'N 1980). The judge, of course, does not have a client; the prosecutor represents all of the people, and must make decisions for them. *See also* Simon, *Ethical Discretion, supra* Chapter 2 note 38, at 1083. Simon gives several examples of situations in which he believes lawyers should forego legal actions that would benefit the client, but makes no mention of discussing the lawyers' actions with the client. As Robert Dinerstein has said, "As for clients, they appear virtually non-existent in this. . .formulation of Simon's lawyering model." Robert D. Dinerstein, *Client-Centered Counseling: Reappraisal and Refinement,* 32 ARIZ. L. REV. 501, 599–600 (1990).

[12] Rhode, In the Interests of Justice, *supra* Chapter 3 note 5. Rhode and Simon characterize their lawyering model as "contextual." *See id.* at 66; Simon, The Practice of Justice, *supra* Chapter 3 note 4, at 9. In an article, advocating a position that is similar to ours, Rhode argues that lawyers should offer moral advice, but cannot impose it. Deborah L. Rhode, *Moral Counseling,* 75 FORDHAM L. REV. 1217, 1331 (2006).

obligation conflict, moral obligation takes precedence."[13] He argues that if a lawyer's efforts to influence a client fail, "a betrayal by the lawyer of a client's projects" may be justified "if the lawyer persists in the conviction that they are immoral or unjust."[14]

The elder lawyer in the segregated-factories story seems to take responsibility for the moral decision, and it appears that the corporate secretary depends on both the lawyer's moral certainty and the lawyer's taking of responsibility. We imagine the corporate secretary telling the management of the company that the law (or at any rate, their lawyer) required integration. Our concern is that the lawyer may have deprived the secretary and the others within the corporation of the opportunity and the responsibility to have their own moral conversation, to wrestle with and take responsibility for what their company would do.

5. CANDOR OR MANIPULATION

Traditional lawyers control decisions in representation through the candid exercise of power. But some lawyers take control of moral direction in legal representation through manipulation. In the segregated-factories story, for example, the elder lawyer might have announced his advice as *legal* advice, rather than moral advice. He might have made it appear that the law required the company to integrate the factories, when the law did not yet impose such a requirement.

At times, lawyers impose their "professional" judgment on their clients, not by misstating the law, but by citing common practice. An example: A grandmother employed a friend of ours to draft her will. She had two children. She had one living child, an adult unmarried daughter. The other child, a son, had died leaving two children (the client's grandchildren). The grandmother told her lawyer she wanted her daughter and each of her grandchildren to have a third of her property.

> "No, no," her lawyer said. "That is not the way it is done: You should leave half to your daughter and one-fourth each to your grandchildren."
>
> "Oh. Is that how it is done?"
>
> "Yes. That's the way."

The lawyer had made a law-office norm out of the old English Statute of Distributions,[15] and, no doubt, he had grown in the clarity with which he

---

[13] Luban, *The Adversary System Excuse, supra* Chapter 3 note 6.

[14] David Luban, Lawyers and Justice: An Ethical Study 174 (1988).

[15] Under the English Statute of Distributions and intestacy statutes in most jurisdictions, when someone dies without a will and without a living spouse, the property is distributed to the children. If one of the decedent's children has already died, that child's share is divided *per stirpes* to his or her surviving children.

imposed the norm as his clients obeyed it. We are happy to report that the grandmother did not follow the norm. She told her lawyer she meant what she said.

In the segregated factories story, if the elder lawyer had implied that the law required the client to integrate the factories, that probably would have foreclosed moral discourse, even the scant moral discourse that in fact occurred. It appears that the elder lawyer here foreclosed moral deliberation by his client as effectively as if he had been dishonest about the law. And this while he set his corporate client on a course that was both undoubtedly right and undoubtedly painful.

6. MORAL ELITISM

Those who advocate lawyer control of moral direction in legal representation believe that lawyers have circumstantial superiority. The traditional lawyer is often candid in admitting that the lawyer takes control because the lawyer enjoys superior social status in the community, superior influence, superior intelligence, and superior moral sensitivity. David Hoffman and George Sharswood, drafters of the earliest lawyer statements on professional responsibility, trusted lawyers, but they did not trust the people. Their faith, as Sharswood put it, was that the republican traditional lawyer could see to rectitude among restless and rapacious clients and thereby preserve the common good: "It is in some measure the duty of counsel," he said, "to be the keeper of the conscience of the client; not to suffer him through the influence of his feelings or interest, to do or say anything wrong. . . ."[16] Hoffman disapproved of lawyers who invoked statutes of limitation or the law of infancy to defeat otherwise valid contract claims. He said of the client who wanted him to make such a claim in pleading, "he shall never make me a partner in his knavery."[17]

More recently, Judge Clement Haynsworth reflected similar sentiments to a law school graduating class:

> [The lawyer] serves his clients without being their servant. He serves to further the lawful and proper objective of the client, but the lawyer must never forget that he is the master. He is not there to do the client's bidding. It is for the lawyer to decide what is morally and legally right, and, as a professional, he cannot give in to a client's attempt to persuade him to take some other stand. . . . During my years of practice, . . . I told [my clients] what would be

[16] George Sharswood, *Essay on Professional Ethics* (1854), 32 Reports of the American Bar Ass'n (1907), *quoted in* Shaffer, American Legal Ethics, *supra* Preface to the First Edition note 1, at 225.

[17] "Resolutions on Professional Deportment," No. XIV, *in* I Hoffman, a Course of Legal Study (2d ed. 1836), *quoted in* Shaffer, Faith and the Professions, *supra* Chapter 3 note 1, at 64.

> done and firmly rejected suggestions that I do something else which I felt improper. . . .[18]

Those who advocate lawyer control of moral choices want lawyers to see to it that moral influence runs in only one direction—from lawyer to client. In the last chapter, we noted that some of the client-centered counselors base their deference to client control on a belief in "the innate goodness of man and woman."[19] Those who advocate lawyer control sometimes appear to believe in the innate evil of clients and the innate goodness of lawyers.

We suggest a bit of humility is justified when approaching the moral issues that arise in the law office. These moral issues are likely to be difficult. People disagree over what sound ethics require. We do not suggest that there are not objective moral standards, but none of us has perfect ability to discern those standards or to determine how they would apply in every situation. The danger is that lawyers will be confident of a moral judgment when confidence is not justified. In most human associations two consciences in conversation will make a better moral judgment than one. We would not insulate the law office from that fact.

Guru lawyers are rightfully concerned that their representation yield justice, but in the words of Teresa Stanton Collett, "recognizing what is just in particular circumstances often requires genuine humility—a trait lawyers are not noted for having in abundance." She learned that lesson as a young lawyer with a large corporate firm. Here is her story:

* * *

> Our firm acted as local counsel for a large multi-national corporation. As it happened, the mother of the general counsel lived in Oklahoma. She was elderly and in poor health. During a visit, her son, the general counsel, observed that she had lost weight and stopped taking care of herself. He became convinced that she was not taking her medication and was not capable of living independently. He asked that our firm represent him individually, providing information about local long-term care facilities and initiating a guardianship proceeding. I had developed a recognized specialty in guardianship work, so one of the partners recommended that I handle the matter. The partner escorted the general counsel to my office and introduced him, both by name and status within the client corporation. At the end of the introduction, there was no doubt in my mind about how important it was that this man be happy with my legal work.

---

[18] Clement F. Haynsworth, *Professionalism in Lawyering*, 27 S.C. L. REV. 627, 628 (1976).

[19] Bastress & Harbaugh, *supra* Chapter 2 note 5, at 57.

We discussed his mother's situation, and at the end of the interview the client invited my husband and me to have dinner with him that evening at the restaurant of my choice. He joked about how young lawyers rarely have the time to eat out, and noticing the picture of my young son, asked that I not pick what was probably our usual restaurant—McDonald's. He took us to a wonderful restaurant and charmed both my husband and me with stories of the challenges his company had to overcome when opening markets in Asia. During the last part of the dinner he asked about my professional aspirations and gave me advice about how to attain them. By the end of the meal, I would have championed this man's cause anywhere and any time.

The next day I prepared the guardianship petition and notice of the proceeding. It was my practice to personally deliver a copy to the prospective ward in order to observe the person. I took the notice and headed for the nursing home where my client had placed his mother after his last visit. Upon my arrival I was directed to the mother's room. I knocked on her door and she invited me in. As I entered the room, she lowered her copy of the "Wall Street Journal" and greeted me. [She folded] her paper and comment[ed] on the increased royalty payments being paid in Southeastern Oklahoma. I felt sick.

. . . .

I did not return to the office. Instead I went home and cried until my husband returned from work. I told him how betrayed I felt—the client was trying to use me to do something fundamentally wrong, and he must have known it or he wouldn't have spent so much time charming us. I felt naïve and stupid to be taken in by such an obvious ploy. I felt scared, because I could not continue with the representation—and I feared the reaction of the firm. My husband listened as I poured out the entire story. After talking the situation through, he asked what I intended to do. I told him I was afraid I might be asked to resign if I refused to complete the guardianship. He said that resignation was preferable to doing something that I believed so clearly wrong.

I doubt I slept three hours that night. The next morning I was at the office before eight—a sufficiently rare event to evoke comment. My senior partner came in, saw me waiting at his door, and said "You look terrible." I replied, "We have to talk." "That's obvious. Wait for me in my office while I get a cup of coffee," he said.

I began by describing the previous day's interview with the client's mother. I said I could not go forward seeking a guardianship over a woman who was obviously competent. I acknowledged the possibility that the firm would disagree, and no longer wish to employ an associate that did not complete her assignments. Nonetheless I would not continue the representation. . . . The partner told me to call the client, and explain why the firm could not continue representation.

I was relieved, but nervous. I called the client's office. He was not in. He returned my call from the corporate jet. While irrelevant, this fact just reinforced all my fears—I was about to say no to a man who controlled millions of dollars of legal work and who probably would demand that the firm deliver my head on a silver platter.

I began the conversation by describing my encounter with his mother the previous day. I told him that she seemed remarkably lucid, and would succeed in persuading the court that she was capable of making her own decisions. I explained that, based on my interview with her, I was unwilling to go forward with the guardianship petition. After a pregnant pause, the client asked that I do two things: 1) talk with his mother's doctors, and 2) go see her again. When I had completed those tasks, I could dismiss or prosecute the petition as I saw fit. He left the ultimate decision to me.

. . . I went to see the client's mother again. As I entered the nursing home, I asked one of the nurses about the mother's care. She replied that the mother was doing well because she took her medication every day but she had been in real trouble when she was admitted. I thought about this as I went to the woman's room. This time she was not reading, nor did she seem to recognize me. I identified myself as her son's lawyer and told her that we had met the day before. She told me that it was not possible that we had met because she had been out shopping the day before. I asked her if she remembered the papers I had given her, and she insisted that we had never met. I then asked about her family members, and she explained that she had no grandchildren (she had several), and her son was an airline pilot (he was general counsel).

Suddenly I remembered that I had read that many elderly clients have "windows of lucidity," or intermittent periods when they are rational and lucid. It was clear to me that this was what I was dealing with. The doctor confirmed this. When the client's mother received her medication regularly she experienced periods of lucidity, but even these were sporadic. Without her medication she was irrational and refused to eat or take care of the most fundamental tasks of personal hygiene.

I returned to the office and called the client immediately. I told him that he would have the order appointing him as guardian as soon as possible.

Approximately one month later I obtained the order, and forwarded it to the client. The firm sent a bill for my services. A few weeks later I received a letter and a check in the mail. The client wrote "I hire hundreds of lawyers throughout the country. All of them are smart. Most of them work hard. Few have courage. Thank you for what you did for my mother and me." The check included a substantial bonus.

This experience taught me many lessons—the most important being that clients are as often occasions of grace as of sin. My client's generous response to my premature conclusions taught me to look more carefully at evidence before I reach a conclusion. His subsequent letter strengthened my belief that clients want and need lawyers who care about justice and compassion. My partner's advice and willingness to allow me to withdraw evidenced the reality that law firms can be moral communities.[20]

* * *

Those who advocate lawyer control of moral choices ignore the possibility that this person I am serving might be a source of morals for me. In the words of Martin Buber, they see the client as an "it," rather than as a "thou." The tendency of an I-Thou relationship, Buber said, is "to change something in the other, but also to let *me* be changed by him."[21] Karl Barth's principle of conditional advice is a good one for professionals: One who sets out to counsel his sister or brother must be prepared to be counseled in turn if there is need of it.[22] Lawyers should be prepared to learn from their clients, as Teresa Collett learned from her client. Moral issues that arise in legal representation are likely to need the moral resources of both the lawyer and the client.

Discussions of professional responsibility in books, law school classes, and bar association meetings generally start with the assumption that the client will be a moral problem for the lawyer, that the client will want the lawyer to do things that are illegal and immoral.

---

[20] Teresa Stanton Collett, *To Be a Professing Woman, in* Can a Good Christian Be a Good Lawyer? 53 (Thomas E. Baker & Timothy W. Floyd eds., 1998).

[21] *See* Martin Buber, I and Thou (Kaufman trans., 1942).

[22] *See* Barth, *supra* Chapter 2 note 40.

Whereas some client-centered counselors believe in the innate goodness of clients and some Guru lawyers believe in the innate evil of clients (and the innate goodness of lawyers), the lessons of our religious traditions, our literature, and our history suggest that within lawyers and clients is a complex combination of good and evil. Lawyers are wrong to start with the assumption that clients will make selfish choices. Clients have moral values and may act in accord with them. When confronted with a moral issue, most people do not automatically make the selfish choice. They wrestle with the moral direction of their lives and sometimes need help wrestling with it. They may welcome the lawyer's aid. Lawyers and clients are most likely to determine what is good if they bring all of the moral resources that each of them has to the search.

7. WILLIAM SIMON: THE LAW'S MORAL SUPERIORITY AND THE LAWYER'S TECHNICAL SUPERIORITY

William Simon's advocacy of lawyer control of moral choices does not appear to be based on the lawyer's moral superiority. He advocates lawyer control for two other reasons. First, he believes lawyers generally will control decisions in representation,[23] and, to use our metaphors, he prefers Guru lawyers to Autocrat lawyers. Second, his position concerning the values that should control moral decisions during representation places such decisions beyond the ability of most clients.

Simon argues that "justice" should control decisions during legal representation,[24] but he is not talking about the client's or lawyer's ordinary sense of justice. He argues that the justice which is found in our "legal values" should control decisions and he proposes a method of discerning such ideals that generally will require legal training.[25] Simon's justice is a recondite commodity. It is within the province of experts. Simon's method of resolving moral issues does what David Luban accuses professionals of doing: It turns all the problems of the client into technical problems.[26] The lawyer makes decisions, based not on moral superiority but on technical superiority. Simon appears to assume, not the moral

[23] Simon, The Practice of Justice *supra* Chapter 3 note 4, at 50–52, 138–39. Simon's early writing encouraged active client involvement and responsibility for moral choices (*see* William H. Simon, *The Ideology of Advocacy: Procedural Justice and Professional Ethics*, 1978 WIS. L. REV. 29, 131 (1978), and *infra* Chapter 6 note 1), but he appears to have given up on that possibility.

[24] Simon, The Practice of Justice, *supra* Chapter 3 note 4, at 138.

[25] *Id.* at 139. Simon suggests that in taking moral direction in legal representation the lawyer must reconcile:

> . . . the conflicting legal values implicated directly in the client's claim or goal. These conflicts usually arise in the form of the overlapping tensions between substance and procedure, purpose and form, and broad and narrow framing.

Simon, *Ethical Discretion, supra* Chapter 2 note 37, at 1096.

[26] *See* Luban, *Paternalism and the Legal Profession, supra* Chapter 1 note 3, at 459 n.9.

superiority of the lawyer, but the moral superiority of *the law*. (There may be a bit of lawyer elitism here—generally lawyer-legislators and lawyer-judges make, interpret and discern the law.)

We believe Simon's proposal places a reliance on the moral norms within the law that is unjustified. It almost appears to be based on an assumption that *the law* is innately good. We think that clients, lawyers, *and the law* are a mixture of good and bad and that the best resolution of issues in the law office is likely to emerge if lawyer and client wrestle with those issues as moral issues.

Ultimately, we think it is likely that Simon's lawyer will impose his or her own values on the client, rather than discern some resolution of moral issues that is set forth in the law. There is sufficient disagreement about the law's underlying values that Simon's lawyer's legal ideals are likely to look like his or her own ideals. In fact, Simon's lawyer is more likely than other Guru lawyers to control clients. Simon's lawyer will present his views *as law,* and clients may not even know that they have other options.[27] We present a fuller discussion of Simon's suggestion that legal values control moral choices during legal representation in Chapter Six, Section One.

8. CLIENT RECTITUDE AND CLIENT GOODNESS

The elder lawyer in the segregated factories case did not involve the client in a law-office conversation on the decision to integrate. One could say that the lawyer showed admirable concern for the client's doing the *right thing* (client rectitude), but little concern for his client's being and becoming a *good person*. People become good (or, if you like, better than they are) through truthfully considering moral problems and exercising moral judgment. What the old-fashioned moralists called the virtues (courage, truthfulness, faithfulness to others) are developed and made stronger through exercising and acting upon moral judgment—as an athlete develops skill through practicing individual acts of athletic skill. Athletes do not develop their skills through being *told* about them. Lawyers who prevent clients from moral exercise—from deliberating, making moral judgments, and acting on them—deny clients the chance to become better people.

In the early 1960s, the law allowed the business client to segregate its places of employment, and it also gave the client the opportunity to choose to integrate them. The lawyer in the segregated factories story may have interfered with the opportunity for the decisionmakers within the corporation to wrestle with the moral issue they faced. The lawyer may

---

[27] *See, e.g.,* Robert F. Cochran, Jr., *The Rule of Law(yers): A Review Essay of William H. Simon's* The Practice of Justice: A Theory of Lawyers' Ethics, 65 MISSOURI L. REV. 572, 582–84 (2000) (hereinafter "*The Rule of Law(yers)*"); Katherine R. Kruse, *Lawyers, Justice, and the Challenge of Moral Pluralism*, 90 MINN. L. REV. 389, 430–33 (2005).

have deprived the officials of the corporation of the responsibility of taking the moral course and thereby being and becoming better people and creating a better business community.

A lawyer who was concerned for the officials' conscience might have pressed, even required, the officers to ponder the matter in moral terms—to lift the moral weights and run the moral bases. This, as we argue in the following chapter, would not have relieved the lawyer of moral responsibility. We do not suggest that a lawyer should go along with the client who insists on taking a direction the lawyer believes is wrong. Lawyers should exercise moral responsibility—of course—but they should also help clients to exercise moral responsibility.

CHAPTER 4

THE LAWYER AS FRIEND: MORAL DISCOURSE AND CLIENT GOODNESS

■ ■ ■

1. THE FAMILY BUSINESS DISPUTE

The following is Rand Jack's and Dana Crowley Jack's description of a case handled by a lawyer named Robert Whitfield:

* * *

> Johnson, the owner of a well-established family business which bears his name, brought in Warren, his son-in-law, as a partner and manager of the business. Johnson and Warren soon had a falling out and Fred, an old friend of Johnson's, helped them to reach a settlement whereby Johnson purchased all of Warren's interest in the business. The experience left Johnson "gruff and embittered." Shortly after the settlement, Warren and Johnson's daughter went through an angry divorce, which added to the hostility between the two men.
>
> Several years later, Johnson told business lawyer Robert Whitfield that he had been "raped" in the partnership settlement and that he intended to sue both his former son-in-law and his old friend Fred. Johnson was working on the lawsuit with another attorney, described as "mercenary, cold-blooded." Several months later Johnson again met with Robert Whitfield and told him he was about to unleash his lawsuit but was feeling ambivalent. Upset, Johnson talked about his "family's affair" with Warren and his betrayal by his friend Fred. As Robert recalls,
>
>> At the end of the story he asked me what I thought. I asked him whether he really wanted to know. He said that he did. I told Johnson that he seemed seriously agitated, and that the litigation would exaggerate his agitation and continue it far into the future [and that] threats are ineffective with Warren. I judged Warren a lonely and hurt person, who would respond a lot more to care and understanding than to ultimatums.
>
> Robert also told Johnson that the lawsuit had little basis, that Fred may, in fact, have been of great service to Johnson in avoiding a long, acrimonious and public airing of family laundry,

and that the litigation would be both trying and exposing for Johnson, his family, and his business. Johnson did not enjoy hearing these things. "Johnson interrupted me several times while I spoke. More than twice we raised our voices at one another. At the end I told him to think about it and if he wanted to talk to me more he could contact me next week."

> I thought constantly about the people and my strategy for resolving the problem over the weekend. The more I thought, the more I wanted it to work and believed it could. I wanted it to work for Johnson because I felt that a man whose entire past impelled him to vengeance might be setting that aside. . . . I wanted it to work for Warren for the sake of his children, who must be suffering from the bitter enmity which has existed between their father and their grandfather for several years now.

Johnson called on Monday and again rehearsed his grievances. Robert told him he could either spend the rest of his life stewing about it or he could move on. Begrudgingly Johnson enlisted Robert's help. . . . Robert secured Johnson's promise to call off the lawsuit, thus substituting a process of compromise for one of conflict. In this new process, assertion of rights would be secondary to accommodation. This suited Robert, for in his words, "I am not a street fighter."

After several meetings first with one party and then with the other, and after a number of intervening complexities that threatened collapse of discussions, a settlement was finally reached. At one point, with $1,690 separating the parties, Robert told Warren that the deal was set. When asked how he could be so sure, Robert said he would bill Johnson that amount and use the payment to cover the difference if need be. The deal done, Robert reflected:

> I have accomplished nothing more satisfying in the ten years of my practice than this. If I were not paid a penny for the work, I would have no complaint. . . . I hope this brings Johnson some peace and that it purges him of his obsession with the financial losses that he suffered in 1983, coupled with the betrayal which he believes was perpetrated by Warren and Fred. I hope that Johnson and Fred can restore their friendship and Warren's children can forget, over time, the hatred which has existed between Warren and Johnson as [Warren and Johnson's] relationship possibly recovers.[1]

---

[1] Jack & Jack, Moral Vision and Professional Decisions, *supra* Chapter 1 note 32, at 89–92.

* * *

There are parallels between this family business story and the family trust story in Chapter One. In each case, the client felt that he had been cheated by a member of his family. In each, the client went to an aggressive attorney who prepared to file suit. In each, when the client was confronted with litigation alleging that his family member had cheated him, he was hesitant.

But the similarity ends there. Ned, in the family trust story, "felt obliged to sign" the complaint, and did so; Johnson, in this story, expressed his reservations to a second lawyer, Robert Whitfield. "[Johnson] asked me what I thought. I asked him if he really wanted to know. He said that he did." The result of their conversation was that Johnson and Whitfield pursued settlement and healing. In the family trust dispute, Ned's brother died after grueling cross-examination (an unusual result, but one that illustrates the great stress that parties commonly feel in the adversary system); the settlement of Johnson's family business dispute may have cleared the way for Johnson to be reconciled with his son-in-law.

2. CONCERN WITH MORE THAN CLIENT VICTORY, AUTONOMY, AND RECTITUDE: A GOAL OF CLIENT GOODNESS

There were significant differences between Robert Whitfield (the second lawyer in the family business dispute) and the lawyers in the family trust, malnourished child, and segregated factories stories. One major difference was what the lawyers wanted for their clients. The lawyers in the family trust story wanted client victory; they sought to defeat the opposing party, apparently without much input from the client. The lawyer in the malnourished child story wanted client autonomy; he was not concerned about the impact of the client's choice on others. The elder lawyer in the segregated factories story wanted client rectitude; he wanted the client to do the right thing, also, apparently, without much input from the client. Robert Whitfield, in the family business dispute, wanted client goodness; he wanted to help foster a resolution that allowed the client to be and to become a better person, in a family and business community that could be at peace.

Client Victory. Whitfield did not serve as an advocate, as that word is commonly understood among American lawyers; he was not a "street fighter." He "secured Johnson's promise to call off the lawsuit." Whitfield hoped that his actions would restore Johnson's peace of mind, release him from his "obsessions," and restore his friendship with his son-in-law. Whitfield even hoped that the son-in-law would be reconciled to Johnson's grandchildren (which may have been contrary to Johnson's wishes). Is this any of the lawyer's business? What of the lawyer's objectivity? What of the lawyer's singular devotion to the interest of the client? What of the lawyer's *role*?

Whitfield did not serve as an advocate, as that word is commonly understood; but maybe, as between Whitfield and the lawyers in the family trust dispute, Whitfield was the real advocate for the client. Being a true advocate means concern for more than a client's financial gain. Maybe a true advocate considers all of the aspects of the client's life, including the client's relationships with others, in determining how to approach the client, in determining, in fact, what the client's *interests* are. Being a true advocate for the client means being an advocate *with* the client for the client's relationships. It is possible that in Ned's family trust dispute, as well as in Johnson's family business dispute, the deepest interests of the client were reconciliation in a troubled family, and that a lawyer who was an advocate *with* the client, *for* the client's interests, would have enabled the client to see that reality.

Client Autonomy. Whitfield was concerned with more than Johnson's autonomy. He was not a "neutral" counselor. He told Johnson things that Johnson "did not want to hear" about his lawsuit and the effect it would have on him. "[W]e raised our voices at one another." Johnson enlisted Whitfield's help "begrudgingly." In the end, Whitfield was willing to contribute his fee in order to secure the settlement. He felt a personal, "unprofessional" investment in the case. Whitfield's end was not Johnson's autonomy, but the restoration of his connections with other people. Whitfield argued with Johnson; he sought to reunite Johnson with his family. He was concerned with more than Johnson's freedom. He was concerned with the way Johnson would use his freedom, and with the kind of person Johnson would be and would become in the use of his freedom.

From another point of view, however, one could say that Whitfield was the lawyer who was truly concerned with his client's autonomy—if autonomy includes taking informed, thoughtful direction in life.[2] Recall that Whitfield did not act on his own; he had long, recurrent moral conversations with Johnson. Johnson apparently engaged intelligently in the discussion of the situations they confronted. Maybe Whitfield had a greater respect for the autonomy of the client than lawyers who lead clients to follow their clients' initial and angriest and most selfish inclinations.

Client Rectitude. Like the elder lawyer in the segregated factories story (the lawyer as Guru), Whitfield was concerned with the impact of the representation on other people. "I wanted it to work for Warren [the client's son-in-law] for the sake of his children, who must be suffering from the bitter enmity which has existed between their father and their grandfather for several years now."

---

[2] *See also* Katherine R. Kruse, *Fortress in the Sand: The Plural Values of Client-Centered Representation*, 12 CLINICAL L. REV. 369, 432–34 (2006).

Like the lawyer in the segregated factories case, Whitfield was concerned that the client do the right thing. But Whitfield was concerned with more than client rectitude. He was concerned that Johnson wrestle with the situation they faced together. It does not appear that Whitfield manipulated Johnson into doing the right thing. We get a picture of a lawyer and client who did a lot of arguing with one another, who had a real and vivid interpersonal conversation. Whitfield says that at one meeting, "Johnson interrupted me several times while I spoke. More than twice we raised our voices at one another." It appears that Johnson talked in earnest with a person who cared about him and his family and in that discourse he came to understand what the right thing was. It appears that Whitfield was concerned that the client do the right thing, but he was also concerned with the person the client was becoming.

Client Goodness. Socrates, in the *Gorgias*, says to the lawyers of Athens, "When you embark upon a public career, pray will you concern yourself with anything else than how we citizens can be made as good as possible?"[3] It is interesting and significant that Socrates said "as good as possible." He did not say "do good as often—or as much—as possible." If doing good is all that is involved, the solution might be fairly simple: We would see to it that our clients do what we think is right (as would Guru lawyers). If it involved moral coercion, manipulation, a bit of trickery—those mildly demeaning tactics might be excused by the worthiness of the enterprise. But Socrates did not say "do good"; he said "be good," and that is a more difficult goal.

A lawyer who is concerned with the goodness of the client will be concerned with the effects the client's actions (and the lawyer's actions on behalf of the client) have on other people, but the lawyer will also be concerned about what type of person the client is becoming during the representation. Goodness is not primarily doing the right thing—it is being and becoming a good person—developing skills for goodness (Socrates called these skills *virtues*). These skills are learned by those who exercise their ability to do the right thing. And, as Martin Buber taught, the moral life centers in relationships with other people; the center of the client's life—the very stuff of it—is in relationships with other people.

Lawyers who are concerned with client goodness will be concerned with client success, client freedom, and client rectitude. Lawyers who are concerned with client goodness will be concerned with all of these things because they are concerned with the client as a whole person, but they will also be concerned with the person the client is becoming as the client is, inevitably, influencing and being influenced by the lawyer.

---

[3] Gorgias, *quoted and discussed in* Thomas L. Shaffer & Mary M. Shaffer, American Lawyers and Their Communities 14 (1991).

3. THE LAWYER AS FRIEND[4]

The model we advance for the lawyer who is concerned with the goodness of the client is the lawyer as Friend. Some have referred to this lawyer as a "collaborative lawyer"[5] (Aristotle argued that friends collaborate in the good.) We are not suggesting that the lawyer can become a friend to every client. We use friendship as a metaphor, just as we used the Autocrat, Hired Gun, and Guru as metaphors. Our argument is that the lawyer should raise moral issues with the client in the way good friends deal with moral issues, neither ignoring them nor imposing their values on the friend but raising them as matters for discussion. Our point of view here does not turn on friendship as a bit of good luck, but on the lawyer being like a friend—as a counseling skill. In the family business story, it appears that Whitfield dealt with his client as a Friend. A Friend is concerned with the other as a person. In Martin Buber's terms, a friend treats the other as a "thou" rather than an "it." Or, in Kant's terms, a friend perceives the other as an end and not merely as a means to some other end.

We use the term "friend" in its traditional meaning, as developed by Aristotle.[6] This understanding differs in important respects from the way people commonly understand friendship today, as we live in what Alasdair MacIntyre describes as a society of strangers.[7] Robert Bellah and his colleagues describe the differences between the traditional and the modern understanding of friendship as follows:

---

[4] The argument that the moral relationship between lawyer and client should be like that between friends is made in Thomas L. Shaffer, *A Lesson From Trollope*, 35 WASH. & LEE L. REV. 727 (1978); Thomas D. Morgan, *Thinking About Lawyers as Counselors*, 42 FLA. L. REV. 439, 453 (1990); Anthony T. Kronman, The Lost Lawyer: Failing Ideals of the Legal Profession 129–132 (1993); and Robert F. Cochran, Jr., John M.A. DiPippa & Martha M. Peters, The Counselor-at-Law: A Collaborative Approach to Legal Interviewing and Counseling 181–89 (2d ed., 2006). *See also* Shaffer & Shaffer, *supra* Chapter 4 note 3.

Charles Fried has used the analogy of the lawyer as friend to argue for the morality of lawyer advocacy. Friends do things for friends that they do not do for others. Fried's "friend," however, looks much like the hired gun lawyer that we criticized in Chapter Two of this book. Charles Fried, *The Lawyer as Friend*, 85 YALE L.J. 1060 (1976). Our argument here is that friends do more than advocate their friends' interests; they are concerned with the persons their friends become. As Gerald Postema has said:

> The impersonalism and moral detachment characteristic of the lawyer's role under the standard conception [of lawyer advocacy] are not found in relations between friends. Loyalty to one's friend does not call for disengagement of one's moral personality.

Postema, *supra* Chapter 2 note 38, at 81. Dauer and Leff point to other distinctions between the lawyer-client relationship and friendship. Dauer & Leff, *Correspondence: The Lawyer as Friend*, *supra* Chapter 2 note 9, at 578–79.

[5] *See, e.g.,* James E. Moliterno & John M. Levy, Ethics of the Lawyer's Work 86 (1993) and Cochran, *et al.*, *supra* Chapter 4 note 4.

[6] Aristotle's view of friendship is presented in Book Eight of his Nicomachean Ethics (Oswald trans., 1962), *discussed in* Thomas L. Shaffer, *The Legal Profession's Rule Against Vouching For Clients: Advocacy and "The Manner That Is The Man Himself,"* 7 NOTRE DAME J.L. ETHICS & PUB. POL'Y 45 (1992).

[7] *See* Alasdair MacIntyre, After Virtue 156 (2d ed. 1984).

> The traditional idea of friendship had three essential components. Friends must enjoy one another's company, they must be useful to one another, and they must share a common commitment to the good. Today we tend to define friendship most in terms of the first component: friends are those we take pleasure in being with. To us the issue of usefulness seems slightly out of place in a relationship that should above all be free and spontaneous. . . . What we least understand is the third component, shared commitment to the good, which seems to us quite extraneous to the idea of friendship. . . . For Aristotle and his successors, it was precisely the moral component of friendship that made it the indispensable basis of a good society. For it is one of the main duties of friends to help one another to be better persons: one must hold up a standard for one's friend and be able to count on a true friend to do likewise. Traditionally, the opposite of a friend is a flatterer, who tells one what one wants to hear and fails to tell one the truth.[8]

We suggest that lawyers should be concerned with the third and most neglected aspect, the moral aspect of the relationship between friends, but first a few words about the other two components of the traditional understanding of friendship: pleasure in one another's company and usefulness.

Pleasure in one another's company may or may not be a part of the lawyer-client relationship, but it is more important than most lawyers realize. In a survey of laypeople, when asked what they wanted in a lawyer, their first response was that they wanted a lawyer who would be friendly.[9] Often, clients come to lawyers under unpleasant circumstances—they have been charged with crimes, someone has treated them unfairly, they are having marital problems, or they are considering what will happen to their families when they die. If they are to engage in moral discourse with the lawyer, they will need to be comfortable with the lawyer. The common word for what the lawyer needs to be is "friendly."

It is important to see this friendliness in ordinary terms, as Will Rogers did; he said he never met a man he didn't like. Or as Mary Chase's character Elwood P. Dowd from the play "Harvey" did; he said, "My mother said to me, she said, 'Elwood, in this world, you must be either oh so smart or oh so pleasant.' I have tried smart. I recommend pleasant. You may quote me."[10] Friendship in professional life, in this ordinary sense, is a

---

[8] Robert N. Bellah *et al.*, Habits of the Heart: Individualism and Commitment in American Life 115 (3d. ed., 2008).

[9] Richter, *A Survey Report: What the Layman Thinks of Lawyers*, 9 STUDENT L. J. 7, 7–8 (Feb. 1964).

[10] Mary Chase, Harvey (1953), *quoted and discussed in* Shaffer, Faith and the Professions supra Chapter 3 note 1, 269–82,

matter of being approachable. We can distinguish the friend and the common perception of the professional in terms of distance from the client. Recall the lawyer, George Willis, who said: "I'm a professional. . . . I'm going to do a good job if I think you're an asshole, if I think you're a nice guy. I try and be as professional as possible and I try to have a thick skin."[11] Lawyers who act as friends will not seek that sort of "professional" distance from the client, which means, of course, that they will not have such a thick skin; they will take a chance on showing warmth and compassion to their client.

The second aspect of friendship—friends are useful to one another—is almost always present in the lawyer-client relationship. Generally, clients come to lawyers because they need help and lawyers serve clients because they get paid. But usefulness need not be the sole end of the relationship. Friendship for Aristotle was dynamic. It began in ordinary encounters, and particularly in the sort of friendships (he called them less than "true friendships") that are for profit or pleasure, rather than what he called collaboration in the good. If I begin, today, approaching my client as my friend because the fee he gives me will pay the light bill, I have, nonetheless, begun a friendship. The advice and concern I tender him may, tomorrow, be not so much because he pays me for it as because I want him to be and to become a better person—to be and to become a better person because of what we have done together in the law office.

4. THE MORAL VALUE OF FRIENDSHIP

Most importantly, friendship is a relationship in which the lawyer sees the client as a collaborator in the good. The moral value of friendship is something that has been neglected in recent ethical theory (possibly because of the modern obsession with autonomy, which teaches that people have to be careful lest they be influenced). The Greek philosophers saw friendship as an important moral teacher. Jews and Christians often use the word "love" for it. Aristotle spoke of friendship as a "school for virtue," a virtue so important that, as he put it, "Friends have no need of justice."

Friends help us to become better people in many ways. First, we learn to care for friends as they care for us, and through them, we learn to care for others. Friends teach us skills for caring. A lawyer who cares for clients enables the client to care for others. It is obvious that Robert Whitfield, the lawyer in the family business story, cared for his client in this way: "I wanted it to work for Johnson because I felt that a man whose entire past impelled him to vengeance might be setting that aside. . . ." Whitfield was willing to give up his fee in order to settle the case. The care shown by Whitfield to Johnson may have enabled Johnson to take a step away from the enmity that he felt toward his son-in-law.

---

[11] Jack & Jack, *supra* Chapter 1 note 32.

Second, a friend (and a lawyer as friend) provides the truthfulness that enables the client to know what is going on and also to know himself. Aristotle said:

> We are not able to see what we are from ourselves. . . . That we cannot do so is plain from the way in which we blame others without being aware that we do the same things ourselves. . . . [A]s then when we wish to see our own face, we do so by looking into the mirror, in the same way when we wish to know ourselves we can obtain that knowledge by looking at our friend. . . . The self-sufficing man will require friendship in order to know himself.[12]

We are likely to become open to this sort of moral insight when we work with someone who cares for us deeply. A lawyer who is a Friend supports this sort of truthfulness.

As Anthony Kronman argues, the advice of friends and lawyers is of value to their friends and clients because they combine a commitment to the interests of the client/friend with independence.

> Friends take each other's interests seriously and wish to see them advanced; it is part of the meaning of friendship that they do. It does not follow, however, that friends always accept uncritically each other's accounts of their own needs. Indeed, friends often exercise a large degree of independent judgment in assessing each other's interests, and the feeling that one sometimes has an obligation to do so is also an important part of what the relation of friendship means. What makes such independence possible is the ability of friends to exercise greater detachment when reflecting on each other's needs than they are often able to achieve when reflecting on their own. A friend's independence can be of immense value, and is frequently the reason why one friend turns to another for advice. Friends of course expect sympathy from each other: it is the expectation of sympathy that distinguishes a friend from a stranger. But they also want detachment, and those who lack either quality are likely to be poor friends. . .[13]

Third, friends can help us to be better people by helping us to determine the right thing to do. Determining what the good requires can be a difficult task. It often requires hard thought. Friends help us in our thinking. We discover the good, with them, through moral conversation.

When a client is your friend, client interest is not so much a purpose as a project. Friends collaborate in the good. If the interest one of them claims is inconsistent with the good, friends collaborate in what Thomas

---

[12] *Quoted in* Shaffer, Faith and the Professions, *supra* Chapter 3 note 1, at 209.

[13] Kronman, *supra* Chapter 4 note 4 at 131–132.

Aquinas called "fraternal correction,"[14] what Karl Barth called "conditional advice."[15] It is not so much that the lawyer's task is to see that the client does the right thing. It is that two friends are mutually concerned that both of them be and become good persons. Friends care enough for one another to confront one another when the occasion demands the painful truth. This aspect of friendship (and of lawyering) is the primary concern of this book.

5. MORAL DISCOURSE AND THE LAW OFFICE

As with the Guru lawyer, there is an important place for the lawyer's values in the law office of the lawyer as Friend, but there is an important difference. Friends raise moral issues, without imposing their values on each other. As Jeremy Taylor, a seventeenth-century bishop and Cambridge fellow, said:

> Give thy friend counsel wisely and charitably, but leave him to his liberty whether he will follow thee or no: and be not angry if thy counsel be rejected. . . He that gives advice to his friend and exacts obedience to it, does not the kindness and ingenuity of a friend, but the office and pertness of a school-master.[16]

If lawyers act as a Friend to their clients, if they are concerned that their clients be and become good people, they will want clients to do the right thing, but they will also want clients to be free: They will hope their clients will freely make right choices. Whether or not a client is free in this sense will often depend on how the lawyer deals with the client. When the lawyer exercises professional clout or manipulates the client to do the right thing, the client is not free and does not grow.

But how does a lawyer help a client make right choices without manipulation? We believe that the answer lies in moral conversation. The professional rules that regulate lawyers in this country encourage such discourse.[17] And many clients want their lawyers to help them wrestle with such issues. A high percentage of lawyers recognize the importance of raising moral issues in legal representation. In one study of large law firms 76 per cent of the lawyers surveyed believed it appropriate to give moral

---

[14] Aquinas, *supra* Chapter 2 note 39

[15] Barth, *supra* Chapter 2 note 40.

[16] Jeremy Taylor, *A Discourse of the Nature, Offices and Measures of Friendship,* 97 *quoted in* Robert J. Condlin, *"What's Love Got To Do With It?" "It's Not Like They're Your Friends for Christ's Sake": The Complicated Relationship Between Lawyer and Client,* 82 NEB. L. REV. 211, 263 (2003). As school-masters, we acknowledge Taylor's implicit point about school-masters. Lawyers are not the only ones who tend to act paternalistically.

[17] *See* MODEL RULES OF PRO. CONDUCT r. 2.1 (AM. BAR ASS'N 2023) ("In representing a client, a lawyer shall exercise independent professional judgment and render candid advice. In rendering advice, a lawyer may refer not only to law but to other considerations such as moral . . . factors, that may be relevant to the client's situation."); *see also* MODEL CODE OF PRO. RESP. EC 7–8 (AM. BAR ASS'N 1980) ("In assisting his client to reach a proper decision, it is often desirable for a lawyer to point out those factors which may lead to a decision that is morally just as well as legally permissible.").

advice to clients; however, few reported doing so.[18] We suspect that many lawyers are hesitant to initiate moral discussions for several reasons.

First, in this, the day of the ten-second sound bite, it is difficult for people to talk with one another about what is good. On the most difficult ethical issues of our day, we rarely see more than what amounts to name-calling on all sides. We see few examples of moral conversation.

Second, the language of autonomy and self-fulfillment gives us little basis for making collaborative moral decisions. We have been served poorly by our experts on ethics. In our popular anthropology, individuals make moral decisions all alone, free—or so they think—from moral influence. We need to recapture the ability to work together, to humbly seek after the good, recognizing that collaboration is difficult.

A third reason that lawyers may be hesitant to raise moral issues with clients is that skills for raising and discussing moral issues have not been part of their training. As noted previously, legal education tends to emphasize "thinking like a lawyer,"[19] more than it emphasizes the relational skills necessary to foster a productive conversation about moral issues with clients.[20] Indeed, in many law school classes clients are almost invisible as the law is analyzed in the context of the distilled facts presented in appellate cases and hypothetical variations on those facts.[21] Moreover, law school required courses in professional responsibility usually fail to deal with these skills. The most widely used textbooks on professional responsibility provide little, if any, discussion of the sections of the lawyer codes that encourage moral discourse, much less any advice on how to do it.

A fourth reason is that the most common image of the lawyer in America is the advocate and raising and discussing moral issues are not a part of the image of the advocate. If lawyers are to raise such issues, they and their clients will have to look beyond the image of the lawyer as advocate to other lawyer images, such as the lawyer as counselor and the lawyer as problem-solver. These roles open the door to moral conversations as a lawyer tries to understand the client, the client's problems, the client's goals, and the possible solutions that might be acceptable to the client and opposing parties. This may be difficult, because the adversary role that lawyers play during litigation and negotiation can make both lawyers and their clients insensitive to the interests of those other than the client, and therefore insensitive to moral issues. As Rand Jack and Dana Crowley Jack

---

[18] Robert L. Nelson, *Ideology, Practice, and Professional Autonomy: Social Values and Client Relationships in the Large Law Firm*, 37 STAN. L. REV. 503, 532–33 (1985).

[19] Sullivan, *et al.*, Educating Lawyers, *supra* Chapter 1 note 7, at 28.

[20] *See* Cramton, *supra* Chapter 1 note 6, 261–62.

[21] Elizabeth Mertz, Language of the Law: Learning to Think Like a Lawyer, at 60–67, 205–23 (Oxford Univ. Press 2007)(discussing the nature of appellate opinions and the loss of morality and social context resulting from abstract legal reasoning).

have said, "[P]eople merge with the roles they play. What begins as a role becomes part of a person's identity."[22]

6. DIFFERENCES IN LAWYER AND CLIENT MORAL VALUES

A fifth reason that moral discourse may be difficult is the potential difference in moral values between lawyer and client. The people of North America come from different cultural backgrounds. Even among the vast majority of those within North America who identify themselves as Jewish or Christian, there are differences in belief about moral and social values,[23] and the breakdown in mediating institutions[24] such as community associations and religious congregations have increasingly left Americans talking only within their interest groups. The internet and social media have simply amplified the "echo chamber" quality of our engagements with others. But there is more moral commonality in America than this perception suggests—enough, we believe, for moral discourse between lawyers and their clients to be possible and fruitful.[25] As we will see in Part II of this book, the moral values that are most likely to be relevant in the law office—justice, mercy, and truthfulness—are shared across different religious and moral traditions.

The similarity between the morality of lawyers and their clients ranges theoretically from being identical to being starkly different. We see advantages and disadvantages for moral discourse all along the spectrum. To the extent that lawyer and client share moral values, there is greater likelihood of understanding. We find it easiest to discuss moral problems with those with whom we share a common tradition—the lawyer and client can point to common norms and exemplars. But moral insight often comes from conversation with someone who sees a problem from a different point of view. Diversity in values creates problems, but it also creates opportunities. Most people have the experience of learning from those who are different from them. For example, when most people view a film or read a book from a different culture, parts seem strange and beyond their understanding, but parts seem surprisingly familiar. We are likely to share significant moral values with even the most different culture. Some parts of films or books from another culture may seem odd but may cause us to

---

[22] Jack & Jack, *supra* Chapter 1 note 32, at 28.

[23] *See, e.g.*, James Davison Hunter, The Culture Wars (1991).

[24] *See, e.g.*, Robert Putnam, Bowling Alone: The Collapse and Revival of American Community (2000).

[25] *See* Moral Foundations.Org, https://moralfoundations.org/ (describing Moral Foundations Theory, which found empirical evidence for five common moral values—care, fairness, loyalty, authority, and purity—that are shared across cultures); C.S. Lewis, The Abolition of Man 95–121 (1947); and John Finnis, Natural Law and Natural Rights 83–84 (1980) (cataloguing many moral values that are shared by different cultures).

question and look beyond our own culture. We can gain insight from those who are different from us.

7. MORAL CONVERSATION AND THE DANGER OF DOMINATION[26]

We have suggested that moral counseling in the law office should be like that between friends, but there are, of course, differences between the lawyer-client relationship and friendship. One distinctive feature of moral counseling in the law office, in contrast to counseling among friends, is that it often involves an *unequal* encounter between two persons. In the lawyer-client relationship, the lawyer is often in a position of strength and the client is dependent on the lawyer.

Some of the most thoughtful students (and teachers) of the professional/client relationship have despaired of professional/client moral discourse. Martin Buber, who described better than anyone the joys of interpersonal relationships,[27] concluded that there is too much distance between the professional and the client for mutuality. He felt that the sides are too unequal: "I see you *mean* being on the same plane, but you cannot. . . ."[28] William Simon, who originally advocated that lawyers and clients resolve moral issues as partners,[29] concluded that lawyers will control the relationship; the focus of Simon's attention became how the lawyer alone (as Guru) should resolve moral issues during representation.[30] Jack Sammons has questioned whether moral discourse is possible when the lawyer and client do not share the same values.[31]

We acknowledge the danger that moral conversation will mask the lawyer's domination of the client, but there is danger in avoiding moral discourse as well. Robert Bellah and his colleagues criticize those who use moral language to dominate, but they also criticize "the therapeutically inclined," those who in the name of respect for autonomy discourage moral discourse:

> Where standards of right and wrong are asserted with dogmatic certainty and are not open to discussion, and, even worse, where these standards merely express the interests of the stronger party

[26] Some of the critics of the first edition of our text argued that the lawyer as Friend is likely to control clients—that he is likely to be more of a Guru than a Friend. *See* Condlin, *supra* Chapter 4 note 16 at 278–95; Sammons, *supra* Introduction note 1, at 8–27. In this section, we suggest ways that the lawyer might avoid such control.

[27] Buber, I and Thou, *supra* Chapter 3 note 21.

[28] Martin Buber, The Knowledge of Man 171–72 (M. Friedman & R. Smith trans., 1965).

[29] Simon, *The Ideology of Advocacy*, *supra* Chapter 1 note 10.

[30] Simon argues that lawyers should look to the law's moral values to resolve legal issues. Simon, *Ethical Discretion*, *supra* Chapter 2 note 33, at 1113. This position is addressed *infra* in Chapter Six, Section One.

[31] Sammons' argument is addressed *infra* in text accompanying note 35.

> in a relationship, while clothing those interests in moralistic language, then the criticism of the therapeutically inclined is indeed justified. . . . But the therapeutically inclined are wrong to think that morality itself is the culprit, that moral standards are inherently authoritarian and in the service of domination. . . .
>
> Traditional moral discourse, while subject in particular cases to the distortions the therapeutically inclined fear, is not the monolith of external authority and coercion that they imagine. Whether philosophical or theological, traditional ethical reflection is based on the understanding that principles and exemplars must be interpreted to be applied, and that good people may differ on particular cases. Nonetheless, there is some confidence that a rough consensus is possible so that there can be common understandings of moral obligations. Not everything is up in the air all the time, although there is nothing that is in principle closed to discussion.[32]

Moreover, if lawyers avoid moral conversations, they are likely to dominate clients who want to have a moral conversation but aren't allowed to do so. This will usurp client autonomy just as much as a moral conversation in which the lawyer's morality alone is the dominant focus.

We, with Bellah and company, see risks in moral conversation, but we see little hope for the development of moral judgment if the lawyer and client shy away from moral discourse. The moral life is, in recurrent classical imagery, a journey, a pilgrimage not without perils. But we think that the greater peril arises from a failure to discuss moral issues. The common experience of the parties to litigation is anger, hatred, and emotional stress. Some decisions in the law office cause people to suffer from injustice, pollution, discrimination, and poverty. These can result from decisions that ignore the interests of other people (and, we would argue, the deepest interests of the client). Thus, we argue that the interests of other people should always be on the agenda for lawyer-client moral discourse, but that lawyers and clients must work to overcome the danger of lawyer domination.

8. OVERCOMING THE UNEQUAL POWER OF THE LAW OFFICE

The lawyer's awareness of the power imbalance, of the tendency of the client to defer to the lawyer, and of the lawyer's own temptation to exercise power, can be a start in overcoming the imbalance between the lawyer and client. We have three suggestions for lawyers who have this concern and want to engage in mutual moral discourse.

[32] Bellah *et al.*, *supra* Chapter 4 note 8, at 140.

The first is that the lawyer seek to empower the client. In the following chapter, we suggest specific counseling skills that can build up the client and put her in a position to participate in lawyer/client moral discourse.

Second, the focus of moral discourse in the law office should be on the moral values of the client. In the conversation we propose, the lawyer will encourage the client to bring all of the client's moral resources to the fore, in addition to offering the client the lawyer's moral resources. As we argue in the following chapter, one means of doing that is for the lawyer to merely ask the client what would be fair under the circumstances. Notions of fairness differ from culture to culture and this question is likely to draw from the client the moral insights he or she can bring to decisions they face. Our experience and observation is that the result of such a conversation will be a mutual moral direction for the work to be done. That is the usual outcome, the ordinary and expected thing. It sometimes involves a direction the lawyer might not have taken if the lawyer had controlled the process, rather than joined in it.

Finally, the lawyer can encourage mutuality by regulating the intensity with which she engages the client in moral discourse.[33] This serves as a substantial qualification to the notion of the lawyer as friend. With friends, one need not "measure words." But not measuring words in the lawyer/client relationship can create difficulties.

If a lawyer is too intense, she may overpower the client and there will be no mutual discourse. There is, however, also the danger that if the lawyer is not sufficiently intense, the client may not take the moral issue seriously. A lawyer can engage a client over a broad range of intensity levels, expressed both in the emotions the lawyer displays and the statements he or she makes. We believe that the level of intensity should vary, depending on the client and the circumstances. At one end of the intensity spectrum, a criminal lawyer who has been appointed to represent a poor woman charged with petty larceny might remain relatively neutral, expressing little emotion, asking non-leading questions ("Has anyone been affected by what you did?" "What do you think you should do?"). This lawyer's primary concern might be empowering the client.

At the other end of the spectrum, a corporate lawyer who has learned that a corporate executive approved the sale of defective kidney dialysis machines[34] might be quite directive (using methods that border on those of a Guru lawyer), emotionally raising the interests of others ("Think what you might do to these patients!"), making a moral judgment ("You did a terrible thing!"), and directing the client ("You have got to stop those

[33] Portions of the remainder of this section are adapted from Robert F. Cochran, Jr., *Crime, Confession, and the Counselor-at-Law: Lessons From Dostoyevsky*, 35 HOUS. L. REV. 327, 391–96 (1998) (hereinafter "*Lessons from Dostoyevsky*"). *See also* Cochran, *et al*, *supra* Chapter 4 note 4, at 181–89.

[34] *See Balla v. Gambro, Inc.*, 145 Ill. 2d 492, 584 N.E.2d 104 (1991).

sales!"). This lawyer's primary concern might be influencing the client. There is, of course, a broad range of intensity levels that a lawyer might express between these extremes.

Note that the factual context of the counseling greatly influences the lawyer's intensity in these examples. Were the criminal lawyer to use directive counseling with the poor woman ("You must confess!"), he probably would not generate moral discourse—he would push the client to follow his wishes. If the corporate lawyer were to use neutral counseling with the corporate executive ("What do you think you should do?"), she probably would not generate moral discourse—the corporate official would probably ignore her. The remainder of this section looks at some of the factors a lawyer might consider when determining the level of intensity with which to engage a client in moral discourse.

Client Control of Choice of the Lawyer. When the client has chosen the lawyer, and can easily go to another lawyer, the lawyer may feel free to engage the client in more intense moral discourse. If the client feels the lawyer has pushed too far, the client can go elsewhere. Of course, as the representation goes forward, it may be more difficult for the client to go elsewhere; there is here greater risk that the lawyer's power will overcome the client. In the case of court-appointed counsel, the client generally will not have chosen the lawyer and would have a difficult time changing lawyers. When the client has not chosen the lawyer or would have a difficult time changing lawyers, the lawyer should be less directive in moral counsel.

Power of Lawyer and Client Within the Relationship. Much of what we have said previously in this section has assumed that the lawyer is the powerful player in the lawyer-client relationship and must empower the client. The lawyer's knowledge of the law will give the lawyer substantial power within the relationship, but in some situations most of the power will rest with the client. The client may have great financial power over the lawyer. The client could be the owner of a large business and the lawyer little more than an employee. When one client provides a substantial portion of a lawyer or law firm's business, the power balance can be with the client, as it seemed to be for Teresa Collett in the guardianship story in Chapter Three.

The power within the relationship will also be a function of a host of other factors: age, education, experience, sex, social class, race, and status.[35] When these determinants of power are primarily on the lawyer's side, the lawyer should be more hesitant to push during moral discourse. When the determinants are equal or primarily on the side of the client, the

[35] Our point here is not to suggest that these factors *should* affect the power in the relationship or that one cannot overcome a lack of power, but to suggest that lawyers should be aware that these factors are likely to affect the level of influence the lawyer will have over a client.

lawyer is unlikely to overcome the client and can feel freer to address moral issues. The lawyer's natural instincts will, of course, be in the opposite direction. The powerful lawyer (with a weak client) is likely to feel comfortable asserting power; the weak lawyer (with a powerful client) is likely to be hesitant to raise moral concerns (and may fail to give the independent advice the client needs)—recall the restless night Teresa Collett spent as she contemplated challenging her client. If the lawyer is to both involve the client in moral discourse and not overcome the client, she may need to act against her instincts. The powerful lawyer may need the humility to respect the dignity of the weak client; the weak lawyer may need the courage to confront the powerful client.

Differences in Client and Lawyer Values. As noted previously, we have proposed that the lawyer address moral issues with clients in the way she would address such issues with friends, in part based on Aristotle's notion of friendship as a moral relationship. Jack Sammons and Robert Condlin have thoughtfully questioned the use of Aristotle's ideal of friendship as a moral teacher in our multi-cultural world. Aristotle envisioned moral discourse within the Greek city-state among friends who shared a common moral tradition.[36] There is a danger that a lawyer who seeks to counsel one with different moral values may think she is engaging the client in moral discourse, when she is merely imposing her values on the client. When there are differences, it is especially important that lawyers make the moral values *of the client* the focus of the discourse.

Danger to Other People. Up to this point in the analysis, the factors we have suggested the lawyer consider in determining the intensity of her involvement in moral discourse have concerned the dignity of the client—the lawyer should have sufficient respect for the client to raise moral issues *and* sufficient respect not to overreach the client. A final factor the lawyer should consider when determining at what intensity level to engage in moral discourse is danger to other people. If one of the client's options will create danger to other people, the lawyer should address the moral concerns with greater intensity—the greater the danger, the greater the intensity. If the lives of other people are at risk, the most directive moral counsel would be justified. (If such counsel fails, disclosure of confidential information may be justified.[37]) This concern for the interests of other people is based on a normative judgment that other people are important.[38]

---

[36] *See* Sammons, *supra* Introduction note 1, at 8–27.

[37] *See* MODEL RULES OF PRO. CONDUCT r. 1.6(b)(1)–(3) (AM. BAR ASS'N, 2023).

[38] For additional discussion of the factors that might influence the way the lawyer counsels a client and the actions the lawyer takes on behalf of a client, *see* Deborah Rhode, In the Interests of Justice 67 (2000) (arguing that the actions of the lawyer should depend on the relative potential harms to the client and third parties and the ability of the lawyer to avert them); Cochran, *Lessons from Dostoyevsky*, *supra* Chapter 4 note 33, at 391–96; Kimberly E. O'Leary, *When Context Matters: How to Choose an Appropriate Client Counseling Model*, 4 T.M. COOLEY J. PRAC. &

9. MORAL DISCOURSE IN CORPORATIONS AND LAW FIRMS

Lawyers who represent corporations and lawyers who practice in law firms face special moral challenges. With unsophisticated clients, the lawyer is in control of the relationship. He or she has the knowledge of the law, as well as the trappings of power: the big office, the certificates, the expensive suit, seated behind the big desk in the elevated chair. The client may want the lawyer to control the action. But in the corporate world, the client is likely to be in the position of power. The corporate officer is likely to be sophisticated and to have the bigger office, the bigger desk, and the elevated chair.

A common question among our law students is whether the moral counseling principles we suggest have a place in organizations. The lawyer may be several officers removed from those who have decision-making responsibility in the corporation. Within a law firm, a junior associate may be several lawyers removed from the client. It may be 10 years before a junior associate directly counsels a client.[39]

The distance of the lawyer from the decision-maker may be further complicated by the fact that the decision-maker may be several people, a corporate board or a law firm partners' committee. When more than one person is to make a decision, it can be difficult to get anyone to take moral responsibility. It is easier for everyone to accept the status quo or to make decisions based solely on profit margin. A further problem is that within organizations, decision-makers are often isolated from those who are affected by their decisions. This distance makes empathy—often the foundation of moral sensitivity—less likely.

In addition, our culture is moving in directions that make moral discourse within organizations more difficult. At the same time that law firms and corporations are growing, merging, and becoming less personal, our moral orientation is becoming more diverse and more individualistic. We celebrate the growing diversity of the workforce within professions and organizations, but that diversity comes with a cost. Participants within organizations are less likely to have common sources of moral values. Moreover, loyalty is becoming a scarce commodity within organizations. Organizations are less loyal to workers and workers are less loyal to organizations. Law-firm partners are less willing to invest time in associates who are unlikely to be around for very long and there is less time for relationships that can be the basis for moral discourse.

CLINICAL L. 103 (2001); Stephen L. Pepper, *Lawyers' Ethics in the Gap Between Law and Justice*, 40 S. TEX. L. REV. 181, 194–96 (1999).

[39] For a perceptive analysis of the challenges of trying to have a moral influence in a large law firm, especially for the junior associate, *see* Amelia J. Uelmen, *Can a Religious Person Be a Big Firm Litigator?*, 26 FORDHAM URB. L.J. 1069, 1092–1102 (1999).

In response to a draft of this book, one of our colleagues, Thomas Bost, identified several additional trends in large law firms that make moral discourse more difficult. Professor Bost spent 30 years in tax practice with the Los Angeles office of a large international law firm and represented many large and successful business organizations. He says:

> Within recent decades, law firms have increasingly been run as businesses, with quantitative indices becoming more important in determining compensation and advancement. Law firms reward lawyers based on "origination" and "proliferation" of business (quantified in terms of dollars of billings). This atmosphere may not be conducive to the kind of client-attorney relationship that could be characterized as friendship. Exacerbating this problem is the increasing proclivity of in-house corporate legal departments to parcel out legal work to several or even dozens of law firms. So none of the outside lawyers know the big picture, but are only familiar with small pieces of a big puzzle. It's harder to have a moral conversation with a client in that context.
>
> But, it is possible. On a number of occasions I witnessed or participated in moral discussions with clients. Often the language used was not overtly about ethics, but called the client to consider the legal decision as part of a bigger picture. "Do you really want to do that?" is a question I often heard asked by my colleagues. What was being raised by that question was the overall relationship of the client with its employees, lenders, community, etc. Short-term legal success might bring long-term detriment in terms of damage to reputation and trust. We often asked the "*L.A. Times*" question: would we (client and lawyer) be comfortable reading a transcript of our conversation on the front page of tomorrow morning's newspaper? As a tax lawyer, I would not participate in a conversation with a client in which the client's operating assumption was that a frivolous tax position could be taken on the tax return because the IRS audits so few returns that the client could "get away with it" (i.e., win the "audit lottery"). I expressly conditioned my advice on the assumptions that the tax return would be audited by the IRS, that, in the course of the audit, the IRS would learn everything that there was to know about the transaction and its tax treatment, and that the case would go before a judge who would also know and understand everything relevant.[40]

Even with all of the challenges faced by lawyers in and dealing with large organizations, we believe that the Friend model is still helpful. In our view, lawyers should treat not only their clients but their partners,

[40] Letter from Thomas Bost, Professor of Law, Pepperdine University School of Law, to Robert F. Cochran, Jr. (July 31, 2008) (on file with authors).

associates, supervisors, and co-workers as they would treat friends. They should have the same sort of moral conversations within law firms and other organizations that we advise the lawyer to have with clients.

We (and Professor Bost) have identified the challenges of such conversations within organizations, but in some respects such conversations can be easier within organizations than within the lawyer/individual client relationship. Lawyers within organizations—both law firms and corporations—often have established relationships. They may actually be friends, whereas the lawyer/individual client relationship is often a one-time association.

Ideally, firms and corporations will develop an ethos that welcomes moral discourse. The corporate scandals of recent decades provide striking examples of the sort of difficulties that law firms, corporations, and the individuals within each can experience if ethical concerns are not treated seriously.

Junior associates face a special challenge in law firms and other organizations. Often, they have little power. They are new and inexperienced; they depend on their employers for raises, promotions, and continued employment; and they often have expensive mortgages, high education debts, and growing families. Moreover, moral discourse requires wisdom, and some aspects of wisdom come only with time and experience. Faced with these challenges, we advise our students to look for firms that have a reputation for close inner-firm relationships and where there is at least one senior partner with whom associates can raise difficult moral issues. Some firms designate such a partner to whom associates can speak confidentially.

Moreover, young lawyers should not assume they will not be able to exercise influence. In addition to sharing with us the challenges of the large law firm, Professor Bost shared an example of the sort of influence a junior colleague can have.

> One time, a young associate of mine (my guess is that I was about ten years his senior in practice experience) asked the "do we really want to do that?" question to me when I had tentatively agreed to write an opinion letter for a client. The letter would have appeared to bless the client's conduct, but would have done no such thing if the fine print were read. The client wanted the letter so that it could wave the letter in front of the IRS and say "Our outside tax counsel has reviewed this transaction," implying that we had blessed a dubious tax result. I initially agreed to give the opinion based on facts-to-be-assumed (rather than the facts that we strongly suspected). By asking the question, my young associate immediately helped me to see that the letter could be misleading and, therefore, we really didn't want to participate in that way. To

raise the question was to answer it. The client wasn't happy. Far from resenting the fact that my associate raised this question, I and the other partners in the firm were grateful to him and other young lawyers for raising such questions. Incidentally, Enron's outside counsel was widely pilloried for writing just such a letter in the company's last days.[41]

For us, one of the great disappointments of corporate scandals in recent decades has been that the professionals—attorneys, accountants, and business executives—who were at the heart of the scandals *were* friends, at least in the modern sense of the word. They played golf and served on charitable boards together, and many had worked together for long periods of time.[42] They had relationships that should have enabled them to raise troubling questions about their actions. The problems should not have cascaded until they required a whistle-blower. It is our hope that one benefit of those scandals is that they have created an atmosphere in which the moral discourse that we advocate will become more common.

10. MORAL DISCOURSE ON THE CLOCK

Another of our students' concerns about the idea of moral discourse in modern American law practice is whether such discourse can take place when lawyers bill at such high hourly rates. It is likely that many clients will not be willing to pay lawyers for extended periods of such discussion.[43] We have a couple of comments. First, in our view, lawyers should not assume that clients will not want to engage in such discourse. To do so would not be fair to clients. On the contrary, we believe that the lawyer should assume that the client will want such factors to be part of the decision-making process. Clients can easily let a lawyer know if such factors are not of interest.

Second, moral discourse in the law office need not require that the lawyer and client discuss Aristotle, Kant, Moses, and Jesus. As we suggest in the following chapter, moral discourse can be as simple as the lawyer asking the client to identify the effects of various client options on other people as well as on the client and asking the client what would be fair. In this way, moral considerations can be a natural part of the ordinary decision-making process.

Finally, in a case where the lawyer believes that moral considerations are of particular importance, she might convey to the client her sense of that importance and enable the client to concentrate on the discussion, by

---

[41] *Id.*

[42] Flynn McRoberts, *Ties to Enron Blinded Andersen: Firm Couldn't Say 'No' to Prized Client. Bound By Mutual Interests and Money, Managers Buckled Before the Houston Energy Trader Even When Deals Seemed Questionable.* Chicago Tribune, Sept. 3, 2002.

[43] *See also* John M.A. DiPippa, *Jacob's Blessing: A Review of Shaffer's and Cochran's Model of Moral Counseling*, 18 U. ARK. LITTLE ROCK L. REV. 85, 93 (1995).

announcing that they can go off of the clock for a while. Or the lawyer could invite the client to go to a non-business lunch and bring up the moral concerns (e.g., the effect of a divorce on the children) during lunch.

As with the other models, there is a danger that the Friend model will foster some misalignment between client expectation and lawyer orientation. A client looking for a Hired Gun who solely supports client autonomy may be frustrated by invitations to consider moral questions that address how decisions affect others. But this type of client is likely to be comfortable communicating that she is not interested in having moral conversations.

Alternatively, a client might not want to have an extended moral conversation about what to do because the client views the lawyer as the expert on the law or because the client believes the lawyer's moral framework should dictate the outcome (as an Autocrat or Guru). In these situations, the lawyer should help the client understand that the client will be living with the consequences of their decisions and should exercise autonomy in choosing among the options they have discussed. In all likelihood, clients are likely to find the Friend to be a copacetic model of lawyer who helps them make informed decisions grounded in the values that are important to them.

In the end, if the client makes it clear that he is not interested in moral considerations (other than those that are an inherent part of the client complying with the law), the lawyer should either defer to the client or break off the representation. Of course, even if the lawyer and client engage in moral discourse, there is the possibility of failed mutuality. In cases of failed mutuality, the lawyer must decide whether to continue with the representation. That is the subject of the following section.

11. PARTING COMPANY?

It is our sense, based on experience and observation, that generally, when the lawyer and client engage in moral discourse, they will walk down a road that is neither solely the lawyer's nor solely the client's, but a road they take together. Nevertheless, at times lawyer and client will fail to reach agreement. In that case, the lawyer generally has the option of withdrawing from representation.[44] When determining whether to withdraw, the lawyer should consider several factors. Moral issues that arise in legal representation may be difficult issues and sometimes equally moral and equally reasonable people can differ over what should be done. If reasonable people can differ over what should be done, in our view the lawyer should generally continue with the representation. A factor that weighs in favor of the lawyer continuing to represent the client is that the lawyer's role in speaking for the client is an important means of client and

---

[44] *See* MODEL RULES OF PRO. CONDUCT r. 1.16(b) (AM. BAR ASS'N, 2023).

community service. It empowers the client and helps the community, in the person of judges and juries, determine a proper result.

In our view, most of the decisions to be made in a law office are decisions over which reasonable people can differ. The lawyer should not necessarily assume that her resolution of an issue is the correct one. The Guru lawyer is likely to have a firm opinion on every issue—we are reminded of the county judge of courthouse lore, who was "often in error, but never in doubt." Nevertheless, humility on the part of the lawyer should not push the lawyer to the point where she cannot make any moral judgment.

As a practical matter, it is likely to be the unusual case in which a client's position will lead a lawyer to withdraw. In part, this is because, as Jack Sammons has said:

> Good lawyers tend to see valid claims of injustice on all sides of all disputes and thus it is easier for them to side with their clients because they know that we cannot determine what justice might mean for us as a community in the context of this dispute without the client's story being well told.[45]

Lawyers are likely to see cases from their clients' perspective and to see value in having their clients' stories told.

As to the question whether to part company with a client, we again think the friendship analogy is helpful. Jeremy Taylor identified "the first law of friendship" as "they must neither ask of their friend what is undecent; nor grant it if themselves be asked."[46] Friends are faithful to one another; they hesitate to part company, and we think lawyers should be that way with their clients. Nevertheless, parting may come. There is the possibility of failed mutuality, of the client's determination to walk a road the lawyer cannot take.

A friend may need to insist, as Thomas More put it, on the little area where he is himself, where he will decide whether to follow his friend. In Robert Bolt's play, *A Man for All Seasons*, More says that to his old friend, the Duke of Norfolk. The pain in his words and in the actor's use of the words shows that such parting is rare, difficult, and not expected. Thomas More was a lawyer and Lord Chancellor of England under Henry VIII. The King needs, for personal and political reasons, to have More's approval of his divorce and remarriage, and all he can get is More's silence. The Duke tries to persuade More to take the Oath of Supremacy, which would recognize the King as head of the Church and would in effect countenance the remarriage. Take it, Norfolk says, for *fellowship*. This is a powerful argument to make to More—a man of strong friendships. Norfolk's

[45] *See* Sammons, *supra* Introduction note 1, at 32 n.122.

[46] Taylor, *supra* Chapter 4 note 16, at 95.

argument goes to the root of the difficulty More is having with the King, who is also his friend. More will not give his approval—his participation as a lawyer in the King's design—because it means something. When More acts, his integrity goes with him. More says to Norfolk: "[W]hen we stand before God, and you are sent to Paradise for doing according to your conscience, and I am damned for not doing according to mine, will you come with me, for fellowship?"[47]

When a lawyer believes the client wants her to do something that is wrong, the moral thing for a lawyer to do is what Sir Thomas More did—refuse, decline, withdraw.[48] But to invoke More on the point is to notice how radically unusual such a course was for More, how earnestly he avoided it, and how drastic the consequences of withdrawal were for him and his client, King Henry VIII. So long as the lawyer does not believe that the direction the client wants to go would be wrong, we believe the lawyer should defer to the client.

12. VIRTUES FOR MORAL DISCOURSE

Moral discourse of any depth will require the lawyer to develop and exercise virtues (moral skills) that will encourage the client to participate and open the lawyer to moral reflection. As Reed Elizabeth Loder writes on virtues for moral discourse:

> *Reflectiveness* is one trait [that will assist moral discourse]. The reflective personality becomes virtuous by criticizing and adjusting comfortable ideas. This disposition also promotes the substantive moral virtues of *understanding* and *compassion* that come from genuinely doubting one's own moral beliefs, their applicability to a given situation, and their impact on others. A struggling moral agent depends upon these others to test moral ideas.
>
> *Tolerance* also is a virtue, but it does not imply accepting all moral justifications on par. Without the possibility of weighing and assessing the relative merits of moral claims, dialogue breaks down. Tolerance requires being receptive to that kind of critical assessment. Self-doubt generates critique. The critique is relational because it involves checking one's beliefs against those of others. If done seriously and honestly, the result is greater

---

[47] *See* Robert Bolt, A Man for All Seasons (1962).

[48] Katherine R. Kruse takes essentially the same position on a somewhat different (though not inconsistent) basis. She argues that a lawyer should not "assist a client *with whom the lawyer fundamentally morally disagrees.*" Katherine R. Kruse, *Lawyers, Justice, and the Challenge of Moral Pluralism*, 90 MINN. L. REV. 389, 391 (2005). She argues that where there is fundamental moral disagreement between lawyer and client, lawyers' moral commitments "carry the unique potential to interfere with their professional loyalty and independence of judgment." *Id.* at 458. With us, Kruse "views the lawyer's moral commitments as part of the package of services that the lawyer brings to the client." *Id.* at 441.

effort to understand differing beliefs in content as well as emotional appeal. Dialogue and imagination help in exploring others' visions. This glimpse can promote tolerance by revealing subtleties and making one's own moral beliefs less rule-like. *Humility* is a facilitating virtue. So is the *courage* to admit personal vulnerability and imperfection.

Honesty and *care* also are important to this process. One must acknowledge that insularity may infect even the most conscientious self-critique. Scrupulous attention to this limitation always is in order. Yet some promise of enlarged understanding prompts hard work and *persistence*. Besides *taking* care, it also is important to care *about* the process and other persons engaged. Much hinges upon this difficult struggle. Diligent striving toward moral excellence is a virtuous disposition emerging from this integrated epistemology. A promise of moral truth makes refined understanding and conduct a possibility worth touching. Reflection and dialogue eventually may reinforce personal commitments. Truth as aspiration may spur genuine moral interchange. In these instances, moral dialogue involves caring disagreement. Inherent uncertainty, however, again properly favors compassion over rectitude. Thus suspension between epistemic doubt and conviction is central to empathetic moral exchange and development.[49]

Wendell Berry's short story, "The Wild Birds,"[50] illustrates these intellectual virtues of reflectiveness, tolerance, humility, honesty, and care in a law office. The story is about a small-town Kentucky lawyer, Wheeler Catlett, who acts as a friend to his client:

* * *

Wheeler started out with a clientele that he may be said to have inherited—farmers mostly, friends of his father and his father-in-law, kinsmen's friends, with whom he thought of himself as a lawyer as little as they thought of themselves as clients. Between them and himself the technical connection was swallowed up in friendship, in mutual regard and loyalty. . . . Wheeler served them as their defender against the law itself, before which they were ciphers, and so felt themselves—and he could do this only as their friend.

The skills for friendship Wheeler employs for his clients are those he brought to his law office from his family.

---

[49] Reed Elizabeth Loder, *Out From Uncertainty: A Model of the Lawyer-Client Relationship*, 2 S. CAL. INTERDISC. L.J. 89, 127–28 (1993) (footnote omitted, emphasis added).

[50] Wendell Berry, The Wild Birds: Six Stories of Port William Membership (1986).

Wheeler is visited by his client, Burley Coultor, an old, unmarried man, who brings with him his nephew and heir, Nathan, and his nephew's wife. Burley tells Wheeler he wants him to make his will. Wheeler tells Burley it is unusual for such an interview to take place in the presence of the legatee. Burley tells Wheeler that Nathan is not to be the legatee; the legatee is instead to be Burley's illegitimate son, Danny, a somewhat shadowy young man who is unlikely to be the farmer Burley is and Nathan is becoming. Wheeler resists. He is, by stout determination, committed to the orderly succession of family farms and to the defense as well of orderly families. Burley admits that his plan is, as he puts it, "wayward." Wheeler mostly reflects and listens. His doing so rests on a settled disposition that is, as it turns out, stronger than his principles.

As Burley talks about his relationship with Danny's late mother, and Burley's injustice to her, Wheeler thinks of Burley's "wayward" earlier days. Wheeler is able, then, out of this exercise of reflectiveness, to back away from deeply held notions of order in the succession of farmland; he is able to be humble about his principles, and honest enough to recognize that Burley, in his waywardness, found a comfort and peace with Danny's mother that Wheeler never knew about. And because he listens, as he listens, Wheeler does what is always hard for noble people: "He feels under his breastbone the first pain of change." He finally gives up his resistance.

His eyes fill with tears, because he understands, and he sees that Nathan and his wife also understand. He looks down at his hands. He perceives, in his client's determination to be finally just (and finally forgiven), that there is more to the moral notion of farm and family and family farm than he thought—as Burley says:

> I ain't saying that we don't have to know what we ought to have been and ought to be, but we oughtn't to let that stand between us. That ain't the way we are. The way we are, we are members of each other. All of us. Everything. The difference ain't in who is a member and who is not, but in who knows it and who don't. . . . I have to be what I've been, and own up to it, no secret faults. Because before long I'm going to have to look the Old Marster in the face, and when He says, "Burley Coulter?" I hope to say "Yes, Sir. Such as I am, that's me."

As Burley leaves, and Wheeler turns his hand to drafting the will as Burley wants it, Wheeler "reaches out and grips Burley's shoulder," and says, " 'Burley, it's all right.' " And "Burley lays his hand on Wheeler's shoulder. 'Thank you, Wheeler. Shore it is.' "

* * *

We have suggested that the lawyer as Friend will (1) acknowledge, raise, and discuss moral issues with clients and (2) not impose the lawyer's morals on clients. We recognize that the challenge for lawyers will be to do both of these at the same time (and that the challenge for your authors is to present a method for doing so). In the following chapter, we suggest a means of making decisions in the law office that we believe can help the lawyer and client thoughtfully address the moral concerns that arise in a legal case.

CHAPTER 5

A FRAMEWORK FOR MORAL DISCOURSE

■ ■ ■

We constantly make decisions that have moral implications. We often do not even recognize the moral implications; we make decisions (both good and bad) out of habit, or maybe even instinct.[1] (A good working definition of a virtue—the virtue of courage, say, or of friendship—is that it is a good habit.) At other times, we are more conscious of the process of moral decision-making, especially when something causes us to recognize difficulty.

Lawyers resolve many of the moral issues that arise in legal representation as a matter of habit, sometimes for good, sometimes for ill. Some lawyers will join in a motion for a continuance for the convenience of the other lawyer as a matter of habit; some will answer questions honestly and fully (without the necessity of formal interrogatories) as a matter of habit. Some lawyers have bad moral habits. (Classical ethics calls these vices.) Some will oppose any motion made by the other lawyer, irrespective of the interest of the client. Lawyers generally learn these habits, good and bad, by observing and imitating other lawyers.

But at times we face decisions that are not resolved as a matter of habit. The issues clients confront in legal representation often are not like the issues they resolve on a day-to-day basis, for which they have an established pattern to draw on. When we face new issues, or when something causes us to doubt our habitual reaction, we engage in moral reasoning. When lawyer and client together resolve issues in legal representation (as we believe they should), lawyer and client engage in moral discourse; they engage in moral reasoning together.

Lawyers and clients reason together best when four elements are present:

> (1) *Client engagement*: Lawyer and client should be partners in resolving moral issues. The difficulty here may be getting the client involved. The client must overcome what may be a tendency to defer to the lawyer, and for that the client may need the lawyer's help.
>
> (2) *Moral sensitivity*: Recognition of the moral issues. During legal representation this generally consists of recognizing

[1] *See* Daniel Kahneman, Thinking Fast and Slow (2011).

how others may be affected and may be harmed by each possible course of action.

(3) *Moral judgment*: Applying moral values to problems and determining what is the right thing to do.

(4) *Moral motivation*: Despite the existence of competing values (often lawyer or client selfishness), deciding to do what the client perceives to be the right thing.[2]

These elements will not necessarily (or even generally) follow sequentially. The lawyer and client may never explicitly discuss each of these elements or even recognize them within their thought processes. The lawyer and client are likely to be assessing more than one at the same time. Each element may influence the other elements. For example, lawyer and client moral values (3) will affect their recognition of a situation as having moral implications (2). Their recognition of the costs of moral behavior (4) may cause them, defensively, to reappraise whether there is a moral issue (2). (One way to avoid the pain of the moral life is to pretend that there is not a moral issue.)

Our outline of elements of moral discourse may seem bookish (this is a book, after all). We recognize that human moral agents do not assemble facts and then apply morals to them (as a first-year law student learns to apply the law to the facts). "Seeing is a moral art." Morals are present from beginning to end. But for the purpose of analysis, we will consider our list of elements one at a time. The remainder of this chapter will describe how each of these elements might be a part of lawyer-client discussions. We will illustrate how the discussion might go through a story about clients who are concerned with a zoning change in their neighborhood. The lawyer-client dialogue in the story fits neatly into the categories we suggest. (We drafted it that way.) In real life, conversation will shift from element to element, and back again, as it did in many of the other stories in this book.

1. ELEMENT ONE: CLIENT ENGAGEMENT

Before the lawyer and client begin to deal with moral issues, the lawyer should make sure that the client is prepared to be engaged in moral conversation. The groundwork for client assumption of moral responsibility should be laid early in the lawyer-client relationship. Some clients are

---

[2] For the last three of these, we are indebted to J. Rest, *The Major Components of Morality, in* Morality, Moral Behavior, and Moral Development 24–38 (W. Kurtines & J. Gewirtz eds., 1984) (a study of the research on moral behavior). *See also* Darcia Narvaez, *Counseling for Morality: A Look at the Four-Component Model*, 10 J. OF PSYCH. AND CHRISTIANITY 358, 361 (1991); Muriel J. Bebeau, PhD, *Promoting Ethical Development and Professionalism: Insights from Educational Research in the Professions*, 5 U. ST. THOMAS L.J. 366 (2008); Neil W. Hamilton *et. al.*, *Empirical Evidence That Legal Education Can Foster Student Professionalism/professional Formation to Become an Effective Lawyer*, 10 U. ST. THOMAS L.J. 11 (2012); Muriel J. Bebeau *et. al.*, *Educational Programs for Professional Identity Formation: The Role of Social Science Research*, 68 MERCER L. REV. 591 (2017).

hesitant to get involved in making decisions—both decisions with clear moral implications and decisions that seem not to involve moral questions. Clients may be in awe of their lawyer; they may assume that the lawyer will be a source of wisdom and that they should defer to the lawyer. The lawyer then will want to make clients comfortable and help them to understand that there are things in life that should not be left to experts, and that the lawyer is not expert about the client and many of the factors in the client's life that should be considered in legal representation. Lawyers can prepare clients for decision-making from the beginning of the lawyer-client relationship.

Making clients feel comfortable (especially when talking about difficult moral issues) is largely a matter of letting them know that the lawyer cares about them as people, not just as a source of income or a bundle of rights. Following Martin Buber, lawyers should show that they view the client as a "thou" and not an "it."[3] If clients do not sense that their lawyer cares for them, they may find it difficult to say what they really want, much less to trust the lawyer in a discussion about moral values.

There are some techniques that can help lawyers to convey to clients that they care about them, but it will be difficult for lawyers to convey that to clients unless they *do* care. Rebecca Howe of the old situation comedy *"Cheers"* (played by Kirsti Alley) said, "You have to pretend to be nice to people. That's what makes you a good person."[4] but we think there is more to being a good person than pretending to be nice. People (including clients) are likely to see through our pretenses of care. We suspect that the lawyer with the poorest interpersonal skills, who really cares for a client, is likely to be better at obtaining a client's confidence than the lawyer who has great skills but little concern for the client.

Sincerity is a start, but there are skills that can help to convey to a client the lawyer's concern. First, when the lawyer meets the client, the lawyer should take some time to get to know the client. Generally, the lawyer and client should discuss something the client feels comfortable talking about, such as the client's work or family, until the client feels at ease.

Second, throughout the relationship, the lawyer should let the client know that the lawyer understands how the client feels; the lawyer should show empathy (understanding, acceptance, positive regard) toward the client. Keeping eye contact with the client and reacting sensitively to what the client says are important.

In addition, early in the relationship, the lawyer should lay out a framework for joint decision-making. The lawyer should make it clear that

---

[3] Buber, I and Thou, *supra* Chapter 3 note 21.

[4] *Cheers: Feelings. . .Whoa, Whoa, Whoa* (NBC television broadcast Dec. 3, 1992). https://transcripts.foreverdreaming.org/viewtopic.php?t=56883.

decisions during the relationship will have all sorts of implications (including moral implications) and that the client will have the major responsibility for the moral direction their work will take.

We can see how a lawyer might lay the groundwork for client involvement in decision-making as we examine the first meeting between the lawyer and her client in our story:

* * *

Ann Welch is a partner in a small law firm in Middleburg, a medium size town. She does a variety of legal work. She previously represented Albert and Jeanie Fagan, the owners of a local toy store, in a fire insurance dispute. In that case, a fire had damaged the Fagans' store, but the Fagans' insurance company resisted paying their claim. Ann did some aggressive negotiating, initiated a suit, and the company paid the claim. Now, Albert comes to Ann with a zoning problem. Ann first gets Albert a cup of coffee.

Ann: How are Jeanie and your children?

Albert: They're doing well. Jeanie is taking a digital photography class. That's something she's wanted to do for some time. Jay and Mark, our boys, are busy playing soccer. Amy is only four, but she already can read.

Ann: That's great. Is the remodeled portion of the store working out well?

Albert: It sure is. We're busier than ever. And, by the way, we really appreciate the work you did for us with the insurance company.

Ann: I was glad to help. And I'm pleased things worked out for you. What brings you to see a lawyer this time?

Albert: You may remember that we live in the Sheldon Woods subdivision. As you probably know, the Sheldon family owned that property for years and years. Five years ago they had to turn it into a housing development because they couldn't afford to pay the taxes. Most of the property was developed into three- and four-bedroom homes. We bought our house when it was brand new. It's the one across from the Sheldon mansion. The Sheldons continued to live in the mansion, but it got sort of run down. Mr. Sheldon died two years ago and Mrs. Sheldon died a few months later. Some people say that she didn't have much else to live for after he died.

Ann: She was all alone. Um hmm. (Pause) It's a neighborhood?

Albert: Right. We've loved our place. It's a real safe neighborhood and it's only two blocks from a park. Some of our neighbors have become good friends and our kids have a great time playing with the neighborhood kids.

Ann: I see. It's comfortable for all members of the family.

Albert: Yes. Anyway, we've all wondered what would happen to the Sheldon place. It was once a great place, but it's really run down now. It's not like any of the other houses in the neighborhood. We've all got new three- and four-bedroom homes, and it's old and run-down, and it's huge. It must have eight bedrooms. They've had it for sale for over a year but I don't think there's been much interest.

Ann: Sort of a white elephant.

Albert: Yes, it has been. Then last week, we got this notice. Mrs. Sheldon's estate is trying to get the zoning on the Sheldon property changed.

Ann: You're upset. I can see that.

Albert: Yes! I sure am!

Ann: The prospect of having your neighborhood change is really troubling.

Albert: Yea. We like our neighborhood just the way it is.

Ann: Let me see the notice. (Albert hands the notice to Ann and Ann reads it.) They're trying to get the zoning at that address changed from R-4, that's "single family" zoning and only members of the same family can live in the homes, to R-1, "unrestricted residential," which requires that the house be used as a residence but places no limits as to who can live in it. You got the notice because you live within 300 yards of the affected property. It may be that the Sheldon family feels that the property would be easier to sell if they get the zoning changed.

Albert: Can they do that?

Ann: Well, maybe they can and maybe they can't. The Middleburg County Zoning Commission can change the zoning, but they try and balance the interests of the property owner and those of the surrounding neighborhood. You have the right to object to the zoning change at a hearing. The notice says that it's scheduled for next month. Sometimes people bring a lawyer to zoning meetings, and sometimes they go and speak on their own. I can help you, either way. If you'd like, I'll call the Sheldon Estate's lawyer and see what I can learn.

Albert: All right. I would like to have you do that.

Ann: O.K., I'll get back to you within a few days and let you know what I learn.

* * *

During this, the first meeting concerning this matter with Albert, Ann has laid the foundation for future decision-making. She treated Albert as an interesting, valuable person; she showed interest in Albert, as well as in the facts of his legal matter.

* * *

Following the first interview, Ann talks to the lawyer for the Sheldon estate and arranges to have Albert come back to the office.

Ann: Good to see you again, Albert.

Albert: Thank you. What did you learn?

Ann: I called the lawyer whose name is listed on the notice, and he said that they want to sell the house to a group called the "Seventh Day Adventist Home for Men." The Home was founded in 1952 by the Seventh Day Adventists. It was created for men who have below normal intelligence and emotional development and have difficulty functioning on their own. It was originally called the Home for Subnormal Men, but the name was changed in the mid-60s. Their lawyer says that residents are limited to men who do not have any history of violent activities.

Albert: I was afraid of something like that. I don't want a bunch of weird old men right across the street from us. Can you imagine what would happen to the value of our house? It's a family neighborhood.

Ann: And having these men in the neighborhood would trouble you?

Albert: Well—yes. We moved to this neighborhood because we thought it would be a safe place to raise kids and now they want to change it. Did you learn anything else?

Ann: Currently, seven men live in the Home. They vary in age from 32 to 75, but tests have indicated that they vary in mental age from six to 11. They spend much of their time doing chores, watching TV, and playing board games. The Home has been located in downtown Middleburg since it opened in 1952.

Albert: Well, why can't they stay downtown where they can't bother anybody?

Ann: I'm getting to that. The residents used to freely come and go from the Home. They could walk to a local park or to a nearby ice cream store. The neighborhood where the home is now located was originally a safe residential neighborhood but has become fairly rough. A man named Reardon is the director of the Home. He has had to limit the activities of the men because of difficulties that have arisen in the last few years.

Albert: They start fights?

Ann: No, but they have other problems. Some local teenagers have begun to harass the residents when they go out alone or in small groups.

Albert: I suppose the men residing in the Home are easy to prey on.

Ann: Yes, I suppose so. One of the residents of the Home was hit and seriously injured by a car a little over a year ago. It was probably the resident's own fault for failing to keep a lookout as he crossed a street; but part of the problem is that traffic is usually quite heavy in the area.

Albert: Yes, I see.

Ann: Reardon has been seeking to find a location for the men that will be more pleasant and not so dangerous. They think that the Sheldon mansion would be an ideal location for the home and the Seventh Day Adventist Church has agreed to help with the expenses that would be created by the move.

Albert: And that's when they went to a lawyer.

Ann: Yes, I think so. The Adventists have a contract to purchase the Sheldon property that is contingent on the approval of a zoning change that will allow the property to serve as a home for the men. It's fairly common for real estate contracts to have provisions like that. It means that if they cannot get the zoning change, the contract for sale of the house falls through.

Albert: Great! Sheldon's family is getting out and destroying the neighborhood. What should we do?

Ann: Well, you have to make some decisions. I would like to describe what I think would be the best way to make those decisions. First, we can identify the alternatives that you have and the impact that each alternative will have on you and others. Then you can decide what would be the best thing to do. How does that sound to you?

Albert: I guess I had assumed that you would make the decisions. After all, you're the lawyer.

Ann: I am trained in the law, and that is an important part of the decisions you will make, but what we do will have financial, moral, and social implications. You know as much as or more about those factors than I do. We will have to work together to see that we evaluate these implications to the fullest. In addition, you and your family should make the important decisions because you will be affected by them far more than I will.

Albert: That makes sense.

* * *

Note that Ann has made it clear to Albert that he should be involved in the decision-making. As clients often do, Albert had assumed that the lawyer would make the decisions. Ann explains the reasons for client involvement in language that Albert can understand.

2. ELEMENT TWO: MORAL SENSITIVITY, RECOGNIZING THE MORAL ISSUE

We will return to Ann and Albert's interview, but, first, we will consider the second element of lawyer-client moral discourse: moral sensitivity, recognizing the moral issue. This element requires "imagining the possible courses of action in a situation and tracing out the consequences of action in terms of how they affect the welfare of all the parties involved."[5] As Gerald Postema puts it:

> Morality seems to require not only that one be able to apply moral principles properly to one's own or another's conduct, but also that one be able to appreciate the moral costs of one's actions, perhaps even when those actions are unintentional.[6]

Ann introduced this consideration into the discussion when she summarized a decision-making method. "[W]e can identify the alternatives that you have and the impact that each alternative will have on you *and others*."

One way to think about this element is to notice that in legal representation, moral sensitivity generally means recognizing the *cost* the various alternatives will create for others. At the time the lawyer and client discuss alternative courses of action, they can identify the effects that each alternative is likely to have on others (as well as the effects on the client).

Both the lawyer and the client are likely to bring particular strengths to this component of decision-making. Moral sensitivity often requires "[f]amiliarity with the situation or the people in it."[7] The lawyer, from experience in other cases, is likely to be familiar with the effect the contemplated legal action might have on people; the client is likely to be familiar with the people involved and their particular sensitivities and vulnerabilities. If the client does not know the people who might be affected, the lawyer might talk about arranging an opportunity for the client to get to know them. Having contact with the opposing party might help the client to be sensitive to the costs to the opposing party.

---

[5] Rest, *supra* Chapter 5 note 2, at 29.

[6] Postema, *supra* Chapter 2 note 38, at 69.

[7] Rest, *supra* Chapter 5 note 2, at 35.

The client-centered counselors suggest that after identifying the alternatives, the lawyer and client consider the advantages and disadvantages *to the client* of each alternative. Under their model, effects on others are considered only if they might affect the client.[8] We suggest that the lawyer and client list the likely effects on others as factors with *independent* significance. This may convey to clients that they should consider the interests of others in addition to their own interests, but we think that is a good thing to convey. Some might say that the lawyer here is "imposing his or her morals" on the client. But we think that the lawyer is only pointing to reality—the effects on others are a real part of the law office decision.

In order to ensure that the lawyer and client have been sensitive to the effects each alternative will have on others, the lawyer might do two things. The lawyer can ask the client to identify the people who will be affected and the effects that each option is likely to have on them. The lawyer can also identify people who might be affected and ask, "Would this choice have any effect on ________?" and, "Would it be likely to cause _______ to ______?" If both lawyer and client contribute in this way, they will put into their conversation the fullest range of likely effects of their actions.

* * *

When we left the conference between Ann and Albert, Ann had presented a method for analyzing the decision: They would identify the alternatives and the impact each alternative would have. Then Albert would choose one of the alternatives. Albert agreed to that method. Ann puts it to work:

Ann: Well, as I see it, we could do one of three things. Let me summarize the options that I see and then we can discuss each of them. Obviously, we can oppose the zoning change before the Commission.

Albert: Yes. I think we should do that.

Ann: Well, maybe; but let's think this through and think about the other options. If we oppose the zoning change, I think the Commission might go either way, but I think that there is a strong possibility that they would deny the zoning change.

Albert: I'm glad to hear it.

Ann: A second possibility is that we could do nothing. If there is no opposition to the zoning change, the Commission will probably approve it.

Albert: That's why we have to go in.

---

[8] *See* Chapter 2 Section 3.

Ann: Well, maybe. A third possibility is that we could negotiate with the people from the Home. If we can think of limitations on the use of the property that would make the Home more acceptable to you, we might be able to get the director to agree to the limitations in exchange for our not opposing the zoning change. What options do you see, Albert?

* * *

Note that Ann does not assume—or let her client assume—that they are going to oppose the zoning change. She lists that possibility as one of the options they have. She does not attempt to steer the client toward one option by emphasizing it more than the other. She also keeps Albert from jumping too quickly to one option. Ann mentions not doing anything as an option—an option lawyers often overlook. We continue with the discussion.

* * *

Albert: I guess I don't see any other options.

Ann: Which option would you like to discuss first?

Albert: Well, I don't want a bunch of crazy people living in my neighborhood. Let's talk about stopping them.

Ann: Okay. In my experience, the Commission tries to balance the interests of all of the parties. Here, that would include the men at the Home, the Sheldon family, the neighbors—such as you and your family, and others in your community. What other people might be affected by the zoning decision?

Albert: I can't think of any others.

Ann: Okay. The Sheldon estate and the home are asking for the change, so they have to convince the Commission that, on balance, the zoning change would be best. In their favor is the fact that it would be difficult to find an alternate use for the home—families these days generally aren't big enough to need a house that big.

Albert: I suppose that's right. Otherwise they would have sold it by now.

Ann: However, the use of the house as a home for men is different than the use of other homes in the neighborhood, and the Commission recognizes a value in having compatible neighborhoods. The thing that makes me think that the Commission might hesitate to approve the zoning change if someone opposes it is that the Sheldons just had the zoning changed five years ago. Did you know that?

Albert: No. I didn't. Oh—sure I did: You mean the change to residential from farming.

Ann: The Sheldons were the ones that asked for that zoning change. We would argue that you bought your home relying on that zoning change, and it would be unfair for the Sheldons to get it changed again so soon. The Commission likes stability in zoning. I think that they might turn the zoning change down, but I want to emphasize that they could go either way. Let's evaluate the benefits and disadvantages of opposing the zoning change. What do you see as the benefits?

* * *

Ann honestly presents the position of the parties but does so without the use of adversarial terms. She does not immediately jump to speaking of "us" versus "them." Nonadversarial language is more likely to preserve Albert's spark of concern for the men in the Home.

* * *

Albert: Well, the big benefit of defeating the zoning change would be that the neighborhood would stay as it is. We like the neighborhood as it is and don't want a bunch of weird people wandering around it. We would be afraid that these guys might attack our children. The Higgins family, two doors down from us, has three little girls. They will be especially afraid. And we don't want our property values to go down. I talked to a friend of mine who is a real estate broker and she said that having these guys living across the street might lower the value of our property if the neighborhood had any difficulty with people in the Sheldon place.

Ann: You mention your concern about the safety of your children. The Home's lawyer told me that the Home does not take residents who have a history of violent behavior.

Albert: I remember you said that, but who knows whether that's enough? They might change that policy. And I'm afraid that the men would scare the children anyway, whether they were really dangerous or not. Children are so easily frightened by strange people.

Ann: Okay. I understand your feeling that the Home might change its policy, and the kids might be afraid of the residents. If the Commission denies the zoning change, you and the Higgins family wouldn't have these unusual people living across the street.

You said you talked with a real estate agent. Did she say how much the value of your home would go down?

Albert: She said that if they keep the place looking nice and there isn't any trouble it probably would not go down. If there are problems, it would probably go down, but she couldn't say how much.

Ann: Do you see any other benefits to opposing the zoning change?

Albert: No, I guess that's about it.

Ann: Do you see any benefits to any other people if we successfully oppose the zoning change?

Albert: I guess my neighbors would benefit, but we are the closest to the Sheldon property. So we and maybe the Higginses would benefit the most if we can keep them out.

Ann: Okay. Do you see any disadvantages if we successfully oppose the zoning change?

Albert: The only one I can think of is that we would have to pay your fee. What do you think that this will cost us?

Ann: As you know, I charge $220 an hour, and, from experience, I would guess that all of the work that goes into a hearing of this sort will require about 20 to 30 hours of my time. So you are probably talking about between $4,400 and $6,600.

Albert: The first time I hired you, I was surprised at how much it costs to hire a lawyer, but I guess I've learned to expect it. We've talked with some of the neighbors and they are willing to help us out with that. Jerry Higgins said he would kick in two thousand.

Ann: So you've thought about the expense. Any other disadvantages that you see to opposing the zoning change?

Albert: Not that I can see. Do you see any?

Ann: Let's see: If the Sheldon house isn't purchased by the Home for Men, what do you think will happen to it?

Albert: Well, maybe some big wealthy family will buy it and fix it up, but the Sheldons have had a hard time finding a buyer. Most wealthy people probably want to move into a fancier neighborhood. I guess the house might just sit there for a while.

Ann: Do you see that as a problem?

Albert: It might be. Someone already broke into the Sheldon home a few months ago, and we don't want people like that attracted into the neighborhood.

Ann: Burglars and vandals, huh? They probably *are* dangerous.

Albert: Right. I see your point—more dangerous than the residents in the Home. There's just no telling what will happen to the Sheldon place. We don't want it to get all run down. That would hurt our property values for sure.

Ann: Any other disadvantages to opposing the zoning change?

Albert: Not that I can think of.

Ann: What about disadvantages to others?

Albert: The Sheldon family would have to wait to sell their house and the men that stay at the Home would have to find somewhere else to live.

Ann: And, as you said earlier, the Sheldons may have a hard time finding a buyer. I understand that the Adventists have had a hard time finding a good location for the Home. They need a large house and they want to have it in a safe community. They've gotten opposition from other communities as well.

Albert: That doesn't surprise me. I'm sorry that they don't have a nice place to live, but I've got to look out for my family.

Ann: I do understand that, Albert. The alternatives to fighting the zoning change are to do nothing, which might allow the change to take place, and to try and seek some kind of compromise. But it seems to me that one of the problems that we have in evaluating the alternatives is that we don't really know what these men are like and how your family or the Higgins family would react to them.

Albert: Well, that's true. I have never known a person like that.

Ann: So, it's kind of hard to determine how concerned you should be about the men in the Home when you have never met them. I would guess that they have visitors at the Home from time to time. Would you be willing to take your family to the Home for a visit if I can arrange it? Maybe bring the Higginses along? It might give you some basis for determining how concerned you should be about them living in your neighborhood.

Albert: Well, I guess so.

Ann: I'll talk to their lawyer and see if we can arrange it.

Ann arranges the meeting at the Home for Albert and his family, and Mr. and Mrs. Higgins. The Higginses decide to leave their daughters at home with a sitter.

* * *

Such a visit can stimulate moral sensitivity. It is a bit of discovery in which the client is the inquiring actor. It will help the client, with his family and neighbors, to assess the disadvantages of having these men move into the neighborhood. It may help the client make an informed decision.

Note that Ann is straightforward about the reasons for bringing the clients and the other parties together—it will better enable the client to assess the situation of the other party and make decisions related to the representation.

* * *

Albert and his family and Mr. and Mrs. Higgins go to the Home for a visit; Albert later comes back to the law office.

Ann: How did it go?

Albert: It went well—maybe too well. A few days ago, I was sure that I wanted to keep that group out of the neighborhood. Now I'm not so sure. You've complicated my life.

Ann: Tell me what happened.

Albert: We didn't tell the kids anything about the zoning controversy. We just told them that we were going to take a basket of fruit to a home for people with mental difficulties. When we first got there, it was awkward, at least for me and my wife. We gave them the fruit and they thanked us. Then they gave us a tour of the place. It's pretty old, but it was neat and clean. Then we just stood around for a while, not knowing what to do. The men look okay, except that they have, well, sort of stupid looks on their faces. And they seemed nice, but very immature. I thought the kids would be afraid of them, but they seemed more comfortable with them than my wife and I did. Our awkwardness didn't seem to bother the kids. Pretty interesting. One of the residents asked if we knew how to play checkers. Well, my daughter has learned to play checkers and she is pretty good. So she played checkers. We all played checkers a few times—that seems to be a big game with them. They gave us some iced tea and we left. What do we do now?

Ann: Well, we have to decide what to do. We have to decide whether to fight the zoning change. When you were here before we identified the advantages and disadvantages of fighting it. Advantages, to you and your neighbors, were that if the zoning change is rejected you would not have the concern for your children's safety and your property values. Disadvantages of fighting it would be that you would have to pay my fee; and the house might stay vacant and attract vagrants to the neighborhood. You also would have the disadvantage to the Sheldons—not being able to sell their house—and to the men at the Home—not having a new place to live. Is that still the way you see it?

Albert: I'm not so concerned with any danger to the kids from the guys that are at the Home now, but I do wonder what kind of people might live there in the future. That's also what Consuelo Higgins says, and I think Jerry agrees. We wouldn't want it changed to a home for juvenile delinquents. And, I guess, I'm a little more sensitive to the plight of the men in the Home—they live in a pretty rough neighborhood.

* * *

3. ELEMENT THREE: MORAL JUDGMENT, DECIDING WHAT IS RIGHT

A third element of moral collaboration during legal representation is moral judgment. Of course, lawyers and clients exercise moral judgment throughout the process of working together in the law office. The decision to consider the interests of others is itself a matter of moral judgment; but here we focus on the moral judgment that comes after the lawyer and client identify the interests of others. Once they identify the interests of others, the lawyer and client determine what a moral course of action would be.

Judgment (what classical ethics calls the virtue of prudence; Aristotle called it the skill of deliberating well) is a complex matter. As Gerald Postema says:

> Judgment is neither a matter of simply applying general rules to particular cases nor a matter of mere intuition. It is a complex faculty, difficult to characterize, in which general principles or values and the particularities of the case both play important roles. The principles or values provide a framework within which to work and a target at which to aim. But they do not determine decisions. Instead, we rely on our judgment to achieve a coherence among the conflicting values which is sensitive to the particular circumstances. Judgment thus involves the ability to take a comprehensive view of the values and concerns at stake, based on one's experience and knowledge of the world. And this involves awareness of the full range of shared experience, beliefs, relations, and expectations within which these values and concerns have significance.[9]

Moral judgment can be challenging in any context, but the lawyer-client relationship adds special complications. We believe lawyers should help the client make moral judgments without imposing their moral values on the client. We do not believe that lawyers should merely exercise their own moral judgment (as when the lawyer is a Guru), nor do we believe that the lawyer should merely follow the client's initial impulse (as when the lawyer is a Hired Gun).

But if both lawyer and client are to participate in a shared moral life during legal representation, they must develop a way of talking about and making moral judgments. Lawyers can stimulate such judgment in at least two ways. First, when clients indulge in the natural tendency to see the situation solely from their own perspective (which generally will leave them feeling that they are being treated unfairly by other people or by a court), lawyers can provide objectivity. Maybe, for example, they can show that the client has been treated like everyone else. Too often lawyers,

---

[9] Postema, *supra* Chapter 2 note 38, at 68.

wanting to be seen by clients as aggressive advocates, join clients in criticizing the reasonable claims of other people or the ordinary operations of the legal system.

Second, during the course of decision-making, the lawyer can introduce moral judgment as a legitimate objective. It is likely that clients will look to lawyers to structure the conversation. We believe that lawyers must develop a way of bringing moral considerations into the discussion, but without controlling the result. Lawyers must avoid the danger that they will make their own determination about a just resolution of the dispute and then impose it on clients. If clients are to fully participate in decisions and experience the moral development that we feel is an important part of the attorney-client relationship (or the autonomy that others feel is at the heart of it), lawyers must be careful not to announce and insist on their perception of justice. (Lawyers often have enough power to do that.) The client must be a partner.

An obvious procedure here is for the lawyer to ask questions and make statements that invite moral dialogue. Of course, lawyers who are skilled at asking leading questions on cross-examination (and at times on direct) can, if they choose, ask clients questions in a manner that will lead clients toward the lawyer's answer. (Some law teachers who think of themselves as "Socratic" know about that.) We suggest non-leading questions.

At times the lawyer can, without being judgmental, suggest moral values that might help to resolve the issues that face the client. Judgmental remarks stifle moral discourse. For this, we suggest, in general, that the lawyer use tentative language.

> This necessary tentativeness can be communicated through words and phrases that dilute an otherwise concrete statement. They include such auxiliary words ("may," "can," "could," "might"), qualifying adverbs ("perhaps," "maybe," "possibly"), and a variety of introductory phrases [such as] "I wonder if. . . ."[10]

The idea is to approach the conscience of the client with care. We do not see the attorney as a prophet conveying the Word of the Lord, but as a friend who respects the client's moral insight.

Perhaps the most common moral issues that face lawyers and clients during legal representation are whether they should take action that might hurt someone or not take action that might help someone. When the lawyer and client have identified the alternative courses of action and their costs and benefits to the client and others, they can consider what action they should take. They can consider what justice and mercy might suggest.

---

[10] Bastress, *supra* Chapter 2 note 5, at 264 (suggesting, in a different context, that lawyers use tentative language).

The lawyer might raise a concern with justice by wondering, "What would be a fair resolution of this dispute?" The lawyer might then draw the client out with further questions such as, "Would that be fair to X?" or, "I wonder what the effect of that settlement would be on Y." Such questions invite the client to see the dispute through the eyes of other people. This concern for ordinary fairness serves two functions in moral conversation. First, seeing the dispute from the eyes of the other party is a way to determine what is fair. The Golden Rule is at the root of justice as understood in the Jewish and Christian traditions—doing to others as you would have them do to you.

A second function of focusing on the problem from the perspective of the other party is that it raises sympathy for the other party. Sympathy plays an important part in three elements of moral choice: moral sensitivity (it helps us to recognize harm that might come to another), moral judgment (it helps us to place the interests of the other at a realistic level of importance), and moral motivation (seeing discomfort in another can create discomfort in ourselves and the desire to see it end).

An ethic of mercy, as well as an ethic of justice, might also come into lawyer and client discussions about what steps to take. The lawyer can invite the client to consider an ethic of mercy by discussing the harsh outcomes that some alternatives might have on those other than the client. In an appropriate case, the lawyer might even ask whether the client's religious values help to resolve the issue that they face.

We return to the meeting between Ann and Albert.

* * *

Ann: Well, we've identified three alternatives: We can fight the zoning change and I think we might be able to block it; we can ignore the hearing and the zoning change is likely to be approved; or we can try and reach some sort of settlement. We've also talked about the advantages and disadvantages of fighting the zoning change. What would you like to do?

Albert: It seems to me that the zoning should remain as it is. We bought our house on the assumption that it would remain a single family neighborhood and it doesn't seem to be fair to change it now. Isn't zoning supposed to stay the same?

Ann: Yes and no. Stability in neighborhoods is important, and that is one of the factors that the Commission considers when it evaluates a zoning change. But they change the zoning when they feel it is best for the whole community. If I remember right, the property your house is on was zoned for agricultural use before the Sheldons decided to develop it.

Albert: Yes, it was.

Ann: I suppose some of the owners of the local farms may have opposed its being turned into a residential neighborhood. But your relying on the stability of the zoning when you bought your house is a legitimate consideration. On the other hand, do you think it would be fair to the men in the Home if the Commission denied the zoning change?

Albert: I guess it doesn't seem fair to the men to keep them out because of something they can't help. It seems that there's a pretty good argument for our side and a pretty good argument for the men at the Home.

Ann: I think you're right. We could leave it to the Commission to try and decide what is the fairest thing to do. We've talked mostly about what would be fair, and that's a big part of deciding what would be right. You've already shown your concern for the residents in the Home. I guess, if I understand you right, that makes the decision even harder.

[Ann pauses. Albert looks at her but says nothing].

Albert, I want you to know that I am with you either way. If you want to fight the zoning change, I'll be glad to help. If you want me to talk to the lawyer for the Home and see about some limitations on future use of the Home, I'll be glad to do that. They might agree to limit the zoning change so that it allows only those with no violent history to live in the house. Maybe you would like to think about it for a while and talk it over with Jeanie and with the Higginses. If you'd like, you can wait a few days and we can talk again.

* * *

4. ELEMENT FOUR: MORAL MOTIVATION, DOING THE RIGHT THING

The question raised by the moral judgment element in the previous section was, "What is moral?" The question raised by the moral motivation element is, "*Why* do the moral thing?" As difficult as it may be to *make* a moral judgment, it may be even more difficult to *do* the right thing. In our zoning change story, if we assume that the right thing to do (the answer to the moral judgment question) would be to allow the disabled men to move into the Sheldon property, the moral motivation question is, "Why should Albert do the right thing?" especially if he perceives the right thing to be contrary to his interest.

At times, moral motivation may be a thing that people consciously consider following the exercise of moral judgment, but more often people probably act morally (or immorally) without a conscious recognition of the motivation that underlies their actions. Even when people think about the things that motivate them to act morally, this is not likely to be something that they consider as a step in a decision-making process. Moral motivation is likely to have an impact throughout the process of dealing with a moral issue. When we have weak moral motivation, we are not likely to say, "I know what I should do, but I will not do it." We are more likely to underestimate the effects of our actions on other people or to overestimate the worthiness of our own cause.[11] Weak moral motivation, in other words, often shows up as a failure to think clearly. "Seeing" (we again quote Iris Murdoch) "is a moral art." It takes effort to be truthful throughout the decision-making process.

Thankfulness and Fear of Judgment. Many factors may serve as moral motivators for clients (and lawyers). Some of these factors are likely to be part of the client's personality or the client's religious beliefs when the client walks into the office. An attitude of thankfulness for what God has given them motivates some clients to do good to/for others. For some clients, a fear of judgment may motivate them to be fair or generous. Clients may talk about these motivations, and we think lawyers should be sensitive to them. They may lead clients to act in ways that will strike a lawyer as irrational. (One of our Christian friends describes his tax lawyer as "tone deaf" to the thankfulness that is the source of our friend's generosity.) We suppose a client's thankfulness and fear of judgment will usually be a given; there is likely to be little that a lawyer can do to affect them. Other motivators that we discuss in this section are more likely to be a part of lawyer-client interaction.

Empathy. Empathy is feeling what another person feels. It is a way to see. It helps us to recognize (to feel) harm that may come to someone else (moral sensitivity); and it helps us to feel that others are worth caring about (moral judgment).[12] And empathy is a source of moral motivation. When we, as Carl Rogers puts it, enter into another person's world, we feel that person's loss as if it were our own loss.

Robert Coles's interviews with children on both sides of the civil rights struggles during the 1960s is a wonderful source for understanding moral action. Empathy's role in both moral judgment and moral motivation is illustrated by the statement of a 14-year-old White boy who had for several weeks joined his friends in harassing a Black child who had come to their formerly segregated school:

> I . . . began to see a kid, not a n[-----]—a guy who knew how to smile when it was rough going, and who walked straight and tall,

---

[11] *See, e.g.,* Paul R. Tremblay, *Client-Centered Counseling and Moral Activism,* 30 PEPP. L. REV. 615, 618–22 (2003). "People disagree all the time about just about every important moral and political issue. But when you parse out their disagreements, it is almost invariably about facts, not about values as such." *Id.* at 618.

[12] *See* Rest, *supra* Chapter 5 note 2, at 33.

> and was polite. I told my parents, "It's a real shame that someone like him has to pay for the trouble caused by all those federal judges."
>
> Then it happened. I saw a few people cuss at him. "The dirty n------," they kept on calling him and soon they were pushing him in a corner, and it looked like trouble, bad trouble. I went over and broke it up. . . . They all looked at me as if I was crazy. . . . Before [everyone] left I spoke to the [kid]--------. I didn't mean to. . . . It just came out of my mouth. I was surprised to hear the words myself: "I'm sorry."[13]

The White boy eventually became a supporter of the Black children. Note that he first found things that enabled him to identify with the Black child—his smile, the way he walked. This identification led him to make a moral judgment—that the child was being treated unfairly (initially by the federal judge, later by the other white children). Finally, his empathic identification with his Black schoolmate gave him moral motivation—the courage to rescue him and to apologize.

Lawyers can listen for, identify, and stimulate the empathy their clients feel for other parties. Clients express empathy for the other party more often than we think; if lawyers listen for these expressions, they can underline them. Ann, the lawyer in our zoning story, did that. She noticed and repeated what Albert said about the people he met in the Home. In Coles's story, if the White boy had been talking in a law office, his lawyer might have stimulated or underlined empathy by showing the humanity of the Black child. Too often, lawyers do just the opposite. They portray the opposing party as the enemy, which discourages any sort of identification the client may feel with the other party.

Lawyers also can stimulate empathy as they identify the advantages and disadvantages of various alternatives. When discussing what action to take, the lawyer can ask the client to identify, and the lawyer can help to identify, the effects that various options might have on other parties. We saw Ann do that in the zoning story.

The lawyer and client can stimulate empathy in one another when they try to decide which alternative to pursue. Not only can they ask whether various options would be fair to others but, even better, they can ask whether the others would find the options to be fair. Seeing the problem from the perspective of the other is the essence of empathy. It is a matter, as Atticus Finch said, of walking around in the other person's skin.[14]

Personal contact between the parties to a lawsuit might help to stimulate empathy between them, but in lawsuits and administrative

---

[13] Robert Coles, The Moral Life of Children 27–28 (1986).

[14] *See* Lee, To Kill a Mockingbird, *supra* Chapter 3 note 7, at 33.

hearings, the opposing parties typically have little contact with one another. Negotiation generally takes place through lawyers. Lawyers often instruct clients *not* to communicate with the other side, for fear that their clients might reveal weakness or damaging information. Lawyers too often protect clients from responsibility for their relationships. The lack of client-to-client communication increases misunderstandings with the opposing party. Neither the opposing party nor the opposing lawyer has a human face. The opposing party becomes an object, a target for anger, for hatred, and for the frustrations that accompany legal involvement.

Maybe one of the sources of the dispute in our zoning case was the fact that the lawyer for the Sheldons allowed Albert to learn of the proposed zoning change from a formal notice that was served on him by a police officer. The lawyer for the Sheldons did not, as he might have, put a human face on his own clients; he hid his clients and himself from the human faces of his clients' neighbors. The problem might have been worked out if the Sheldons had talked to Albert and his neighbors about the problem they were having in selling their house.

Maybe lawyers and clients should look for settings in which the opposing parties can talk to one another. This might be risky: If the parties are angry, contact in the wrong setting can increase hostility. (We are reminded of the case in which a mother attempted to run a father over with her car when bringing the children for visitation.) But we do not claim that moral courses of action are without risk. We do claim that stories, human experience, observation, and the modern literature of mediation all suggest that the hostility that may accompany a face-to-face encounter is likely to be followed by person-to-person communication and understanding.

In our zoning story, Ann sees an opportunity for such contact. She suggests, and later arranges, a meeting between the Fagans, the Higginses, and the men at the Home. The meeting puts a human face on the men at the Home—the Fagans can no longer deal with them as objects; they are now people. The meeting not only shows the Fagans that these men are not dangerous, and that the Fagan children will not be afraid of them, it stimulates empathy.

Ann might also have suggested mediation. If the parties share a common religious perspective, this mediation might occur through a church or synagogue. Mediation through community programs is another possibility. The benefit of mediation is that the parties, with some frequency, have face-to-face contact with one another, along with the help of a concerned third party neutral to facilitate the conversation. Each party has the opportunity to tell his or her story. The setting encourages the parties to listen to one another. The critical moment in a mediation occurs when the party who is talking shifts the direction of his or her remarks from the mediator to the other party—and when it becomes evident that the other party hears what is being said. Mediation succeeds because the parties come to communicate with one another and are then more likely to grow to empathize with one another.

Anything that the lawyer can do to put a human face on the other party, through accurately describing the situation of the other party, or through encouraging the use of dispute resolution mechanisms that bring the parties together, can stimulate empathy and may lead to the client's treating the other party with justice or even with mercy.

It might be argued that attempts on the part of the lawyer to stimulate empathy are manipulative. We believe, to the contrary, that enabling the client to see the opposing party as he or she really is gives the client an accurate picture of the dispute. Litigation or negotiation strategies that keep the parties separate, that always portray the opposing party as the bad guy, distort reality.

Models and Stories. Though we have spent a substantial portion of this book discussing moral principles, moral behavior is more likely to be a matter of imitating those we admire than of obeying moral principles. And it is an ordinary thing for lawyers to engage the interest of their clients with stories of other clients.

One of the children who most surprised Robert Coles, in his interviews with the children of the 1960s civil rights conflict, was Ruby Bridges, a little Black girl, who, week after week, went through crowds of angry Whites to her school. Ruby said that each night she prayed that God would forgive the angry crowds of White people who jeered and threatened her as she went to school.

> Ruby was picking up phrases, admonitions, statements ritually expressed, bits and pieces of sermons emotionally delivered. . . . She was being psychologically imitative. . . . She did what she was told. . . . holding on for dear life with brave smiles and silence outside and inside school, and with prayers at home. . . .[15]

Dr. Coles at first attributed Ruby's courage to a sort of childish reflex—not to her moral maturity. When (at the urging of his wife) Coles focused instead on the child's *acts*, "the *deeds* they managed," he discovered the moral models who had been available to Ruby and that had borne her through hate and danger: "Rosa Parks, a seamstress, whose decision to sit where she pleased on a Montgomery, Alabama, bus in the middle 1950s preceded the emergence of the so-called civil rights movement"; Dr. Martin Luther King, Jr., and the Rev. Ralph Abernathy; the college students who "sat in" in segregated public places in the 1960s—"young leaders of a

[15] Coles, *supra* Chapter 5 note 13, at 23.

changing South, young *moral* leaders."[16] Today, moral models include Ruby Bridges.

Maybe even a *lawyer* can serve as a model for a client. The way clients observe their lawyer treating them and others has an impact on clients. It will probably be difficult for a lawyer to invite a client to follow an ethic that involves sacrifice unless the lawyer is a person who makes sacrifices. If the lawyer treats the client with mercy, the client is more likely to treat others with mercy. Recall, for example, the story of the family business dispute (the lawyer as friend) in Chapter Four. The lawyer, Robert Whitfield, was willing to give up his fee in order to enable the parties to settle. No doubt his example had an impact on the parties to the suit. His willingness to sacrifice may have enabled the parties to reconcile.

Persuasion. In the story of the family business dispute it appears that, in addition to serving as a model, Robert Whitfield persuaded his client, Johnson, to settle. Advocates of client autonomy are likely to see lawyer persuasion as inherently overreaching, and we recognize that danger. Nevertheless, we see a place in lawyer-client discourse for lawyer persuasion, though the line between persuasion and imposition will vary from client to client and it may be hard to identify. The lawyer's goal should be to enable the client to think clearly about the moral implications of what the lawyer and client are doing together.

In the family business story, it could be that Whitfield stepped over the line from persuading to imposing settlement on Johnson, but we cannot know that from the outside. We suspect that Whitfield was able to recognize the line; he was with his client when the line appeared—and it probably appeared to both of them. It seems that both Whitfield and Johnson wrestled intelligently with the moral issue.

In the story of the Home for Men, when Albert walked in with his zoning problem, Ann could have followed any of the models we discussed in Part One of this book. As Autocrat, she could have taken control of the representation and fought the zoning change. As Hired Gun, she could have reinforced Albert's attention on the consequences to him of a zoning change and come out firing. As Guru, she might have concluded that allowing the zoning change would have been the right thing to do and pressed Albert not to oppose it.

In our story, Ann acted as Friend; she and Albert wrestled with the moral issue. (1) Ann kept Albert involved in the decision-making process (client engagement); (2) they identified the costs that his alternatives would have, not only to himself, but to others (moral sensitivity); (3) they tried to determine what would be fair and caring (moral judgment); and (4) Albert met with the men at the home and developed an empathy for them

---

[16] *Id.* at 25–26.

that led him to a concern with what would happen to them (moral motivation).

We ended the story with Albert wrestling with what he should do and Ann's affirmation that she was with him either way. We could include Albert's decision to seek some sort of settlement or his decision to fight the zoning change. But our story is not the story of Albert's decision; it is the story of the way that he and Ann wrestled with it. We think that what he decides is important—important for Albert, his family, his neighbors, and for the men in the Home. But we feel that as important as the ultimate decision is the way that it is made. If Albert has wrestled with this decision honestly, and it appears that he has, it will be an occasion for moral growth, an opportunity for him to become a better person.

PART TWO

MORAL VALUES FOR THE LAW OFFICE

CHAPTER 6

WHOSE MORAL VALUES? WHAT MORAL VALUES?

■ ■ ■

Each of the four lawyers we described in Part One wants something different for his or her client. The lawyer as Autocrat wants client victory, the lawyer as Hired Gun wants client autonomy, the lawyer as Guru wants client rectitude, and the lawyer as Friend wants client goodness. Each of the lawyers has a different combination of answers to two questions: (1) Who controls the representation? and (2) Do the interests of those other than the client matter? The lawyer as Autocrat controls the choices and ignores the interests of others. The lawyer as Hired Gun leaves control to the client and also ignores the interests of others. The lawyer as Guru controls moral choices in light of what the lawyer perceives to be justice and the interests of others. The lawyer as Friend recognizes and, if need be, raises moral issues and resolves them in conversation with the client. The lawyer as Friend has a law office with room for the moral life of both client and lawyer.

So far, we have not considered the specific moral values that might inform law office decisions. This part of this book discusses some of these moral values.

1. "LEGAL VALUES" AS A SOURCE OF MORAL VALUES

William Simon suggests that lawyers should use "legal values"[1] to resolve moral issues during representation. Legal values are "substantive principles that prescribe the just ordering of the social world."[2] He

[1] Simon, The Practice of Justice, *supra* Chapter 3 note 4, at 138. Simon says that his proposal differs from many critiques of prevalent legal ethics doctrine that appeal to moral concerns outside the legal system against values associated with the legal role. *Id.* at 16–17.

In an earlier (1978) law review article, Simon took a position that is much like our position. He argued for what he called "non-professional advocacy":

> The foundation principle of non-professional advocacy is that the problems of advocacy be treated as a matter of *personal* ethics. . . . [P]ersonal ethics require that individuals take responsibility for the consequences of their decisions. They cannot defer to institutions with autonomous ethical momentum.

Simon, *The Ideology of Advocacy*, *supra* Chapter 1 note 10, at 29. *See also*, Thomas L. Shaffer, *Jews, Christians, Lawyers, and Money*, 25 VT. L. REV. 451 (2001).

[2] Simon, The Practice of Justice, *supra* Chapter 3 note 4 at 82.

identifies several substantive theories of law on which the lawyer might draw, including libertarianism, utilitarianism, wealth maximization, liberalism, and virtue ethics.[3]

Simon argues that legal values should control both whom lawyers represent and how lawyers choose to represent them. As an example, Simon applauded the decision of the Washington, D.C., law firm, Covington and Burling, to stop representing the government-owned South African Airways, on the assumption that the firm dropped this corporate client because "South African Airways [was] implicated in the [old] South African system of racial subordination."[4] Simon said that Covington and Burling's refusal to represent South African Airways was justified because the activities of South African Airways supported "a system that violates some of the most fundamental norms of our legal culture [those contained in our domestic equal protection laws]."[5]

In theory, at least, Simon's method would avoid some of the problems of the adversary ethic: Lawyers would not attack others unless they could do so based on the values found in "the law." Resolving issues based on legal values would also avoid the untidiness of lawyers and clients having to discuss moral issues (or, at least, having to *call* them moral issues). Simon argues that lawyers are more likely to bring legal values to bear on moral issues than they are to bring mere moral values to bear on legal issues. His program attempts to avoid the subjectivity that many see in a notion such as "moral values."[6]

There are, however, some significant problems with using legal values as the basis for resolving moral issues in legal representation. First, it is unlikely that legal values will provide a clear resolution of moral issues that the law does not resolve, whether we look at the language of statutes and cases or the underlying philosophy of the law. The law often merely covers over moral controversy. Where there is relevant law, it is often the product of judges or legislators who disagreed on the moral values they brought to their governmental tasks. Legislators resolve issues about which they can agree; they are often silent or vague concerning issues on which they cannot agree (and they leave lawyers and judges to discern legislative "intent"). Issues on which the legislature is silent or vague are likely to be the issues that lawyer and client must resolve. Discerning legal values under the "substantive principles that prescribe the just ordering of the social world" is likely to be equally difficult, in light of all of the very

---

[3] *Id.*

[4] Simon, *Ethical Discretion*, *supra* Chapter 2 note 38, at 1094–95.

[5] *Id.* at 1095.

[6] *Id.* at 1113–14

different potential sources of those principles.[7] It is likely to be impossible to get a clear answer from legal values.

Second, is the law the best source of moral values? Lawyers will find not only many different (often conflicting) legal values in the law, but some values that are destructive. In the early 1990s, the legal value of equal protection might have led Covington and Burling to withdraw from representation of South African Airways; in the early 1960s, the legal value of segregation might have led Covington and Burling to represent more devious clients.

As Martin Luther King and many of our moral heroes have taught us, moral values are *more important* than legal values. In his "Letter from Birmingham City Jail," King declared that a "just law is a manmade code that squares with the moral law or the law of God."[8] For Dr. King the moral law stood in judgment of legal values. King and his lawyers used and influenced the law, but there was never much doubt that their moral direction came from elsewhere. At times, their moral values led them to violate the law. Through its history, American law has at various times supported slavery, segregation, exploitation of immigrants, suppression of organized labor, neglect of the poor, paternalism, and imperialism. We suggest that decisions during legal representation should not be based on such values, nor on their modern counterparts.[9]

Third, reliance on legal values may encourage litigation; legal values can corrode and destroy human relationships. The clients in the family trust and family business stories (from Chapters One and Four) came to lawyers because they felt that they had been cheated. Their question was whether they should pursue litigation and risk dividing their families. If their lawyers had looked to legal values, they would have said "Sue! The law provides litigation as a means of determining the truth and resolving disputes." The moral values of care, mercy, and reconciliation often reach beyond legal values. These values might lead clients to resolve disputes by means other than litigation, or even to yield their rights, because there is something in their morality that is more important than legal rights. In Chapter Eight, we will consider the lessons of these values for legal representation.

Fourth, applying a set of legal standards that are different from the ordinary morals of client and lawyer removes from them responsibility for

---

7 *See* the range of sources cited by Simon *supra* at text accompanying Chapter 6 note 3.

8 Martin Luther King, Jr., "Letter from Birmingham City Jail," *in* A Testament of Hope: The Essential Writings of Martin Luther King, Jr. (James M. Washington ed., 1986), *quoted in* Stephen L. Carter, The Culture of Disbelief 38 (1993).

9 Simon apparently would agree with us in some cases. Despite his call for lawyers to resolve moral issues based on legal values, Simon suggests that in some cases, "fundamental values" or natural law values might trump legal values. Simon, *Ethical Discretion, supra* Chapter 2 note 38, at 1106–07, 1115.

moral discernment. As they determine what they should talk about, and how they should deal with one another, lawyers and clients should not evade or smother their most immediate sources of moral value.

Fifth, looking to "legal values" rather than "moral values" tends to denigrate moral values and is likely to accelerate the tendency which Americans have always both encouraged and lamented to look to the law as the *only* source of moral values. According to Simon, "The tools offered in popular culture for considering moral problems seem too formless and subjective; those offered by academic philosophy seem too abstract and multifarious."[10] If Simon is right, neither our popular culture nor our teachers of moral philosophy have served us well. The moral sense in an individual will atrophy if it is not exercised; we fear that the moral sense of a community will atrophy if it is not exercised. We need to rediscover the ability to talk about moral values, not substitute legal values for them.

Finally, as we noted in Chapter Three, Section Seven, we believe that under Simon's proposal, in many cases the indeterminacy of legal values will result in the lawyer imposing the lawyer's values on the client. This need not come from any sort of sinister motive on the part of the lawyer. When lawyers look for the "substantive principles that prescribe the just ordering of the social world" they are likely to find their own values. "It will not necessarily be legal ideals that control the client; it is likely to be the lawyer's ideals."[11] As Katherine Kruse has noted, a lawyer's "understanding and interpretation of the fundamental principles of law would inevitably be shaped by his moral views."[12]

Kruse illustrates the ways that Simon's lawyer might handle representation of clients with whom he is in fundamental moral disagreement. She envisions a lesbian couple several years ago who are interested in together adopting a child, in the face of a statute that allows only heterosexual married couples and single people to adopt. They go to a lawyer who sees the traditional family as an important social institution and believes that children are better off raised by heterosexual married couples. "He would see the narrow construction of the adoption statute as properly protecting children from exactly the type of legal manipulation of the family that [the lesbian couple] is trying to undertake."[13] Whereas most socially conservative Guru (our term) lawyers would give the clients "a lecture on morality and [show] them the door," Simon's Guru lawyer "would tell them that [their proposed adoption] was not legally possible. . . [T]he legal authority with which [Simon's] lawyer would speak would leave them with little motivation to seek a second opinion from a lawyer more

[10] *See* Simon, The Practice of Justice, *supra* Chapter 3 note 4, at 18.

[11] Cochran, *The Rule of Law(yers), supra* Chapter 3 note 27, at 584.

[12] Kruse, *Lawyers, Justice, and the Challenge of Moral Pluralism, supra* Chapter 3 note 27, at 430.

[13] Id. at 432.

sympathetic to their situation."[14] Whatever the lawyer believes about the merits of the lesbian couple's claim, at a minimum the lawyer should inform them that they might have a claim and that another lawyer might be willing to represent them.

2. CONVENTIONAL MORAL VALUES

Another potential basis for resolving moral issues in representation is conventional morality—the moral views generally held within "society."[15] But conventional values as a basis for resolving moral issues during representation are problematic for many of the reasons that legal values are problematic. Like legal values, conventional values are likely to be difficult to discern and likely to be in conflict with one another. Also like legal values, some conventional values may not be the best moral values. "Society," as well as the law, has approved and supported great evils. As Reed Elizabeth Loder has said, "[Conventionalism] preserves no extrinsic standard for evaluating moral judgments that are pervasive but intuitively wrong. Slavery, Nazism, and the practice of killing girl babies in China all present this difficulty."[16] And, like legal values, conventional values would be likely to result in litigation—which functions as the default way we resolve disputes in our society. Reliance on conventional values would withdraw from the lawyer and client the responsibility of discerning moral direction.

---

[14] *Id.* at 433. According to Kruse, in this fact situation if the socially conservative lawyer acted under our Friend model, he "would approach the moral questions with humility and would be open to changing his views through moral dialogue. . . [H]e would not be as quick to show them the door and instead would be more likely to welcome the opportunity for the moral growth—both theirs and his own—that having clients with such different values would present." *Id.* at 438. Nevertheless, "it is probable that moral dialogue would simply break down." *Id.* at 439.

> [The Friend lawyer] would probably decline to represent [them]. However, the reasons for declining representation are neither as judgmental as those of the moral activist nor as comfortably authoritative as those of [Simon's] contextual lawyer. Instead, [the Friend lawyer] would probably feel a tinge of regret that he was unable to reach a common moral ground with [the couple] or that, in their determination to walk their chosen road, they missed an opportunity to seek the path of goodness that would make them better people.
>
> . . . Even if we believe, as Shaffer and Cochran suggest, that underneath our moral plurality a level of shared values exists, the law-office context seems ill suited to moral conversations of the depth required to reconcile sharply divergent moral views. *Id.* at 440.

According to Kruse, a socially conservative Hired Gun (our term) lawyer would be willing to aggressively pursue the rights of the couple, though it "would likely be experienced by him as a betrayal of his own ideals." *Id.* at 419. "The implicit pressure to default to legal interests presented by such limited counseling may allow [the couple] to avoid confronting their own ambivalence and making a choice that is fully consistent with their values." *Id.* at 420–21.

Kruse argues that lawyers that have fundamental moral disagreements with their clients should withdraw from representation on the basis of a moral conflict of interest that is likely to affect their counseling and representation. She sees withdrawal in such circumstances as "not merely a matter of lawyers' autonomy but, in some cases, as a professional obligation." *Id.* at 454. We agree that the lawyer should withdraw under such circumstances, though on different grounds than those suggested by Kruse. *See supra*, Chapter 4, Section 11.

[15] *See* Loder, *supra* Chapter 4 note 49, at 134–34.

[16] *Id.* at 125, n.140.

3. THE STARTING PLACE: THE MORAL VALUES THAT CLIENTS AND LAWYERS HAVE

We turn now to our argument that clients and lawyers should resolve the moral direction of legal representation from the moral values that each of them has and both of them have. That is not to say that client and lawyer moral values will always be right. Client and lawyer may—they probably will—share many of the prejudices of the law and of their community. But their values are a starting place that is immediate and deeper than what they think they can figure out from the law or from "society." What we are after is an immediate, available place from which moral understanding can be shared and can grow.

Using one's own moral values in a conversation with one's lawyer or one's client is also the functional thing to do: These are the values that cling most stubbornly and wake you up in the middle of the night. They are the values that run deepest and most broadly. They are the values that might cause clients and lawyers to resist their selfish personal interests.

A concern for personal integrity also would argue that people have a responsibility to determine what is right; to develop, examine, discipline, and apply immediate moral values. Part of that (as the proponents of autonomy say) is determining what values we should have, but more often it is a matter of identifying moral values in our traditions and determining how the values that we have might apply to the situations that we confront. An important and generally neglected starting place for discussion of morality in legal representation is: "What moral values do clients (and lawyers) have?"

Though surveys show that in the United States, in recent decades, those who identify themselves as having no religion have increased,[17] studies find that most Americans believe in God and consider religion an important part of their lives. Over eighty percent of Americans believe in God;[18] seventy-five percent claim affiliation with organized religion (sixty-eight percent Christian);[19] and more than six in ten Americans pray (though more often in their cars than in places of worship).[20]

---

[17] The Pew Forum on Religion & Public Life, *America's Changing Religious Landscape* (May 12, 2015), https://www.pewresearch.org/wp-content/uploads/sites/20/2015/05/RLS-08-26-full-report.pdf. The number of those unaffiliated with any religious group rose from 16.1% in 2007 to 22.8% in 2014. *Id.* at 30.

[18] *How Many Americans Believe in God?*, GALLUP (June 24, 2022), https://news.gallup.com/poll/268205/americans-believe-god.aspx.

[19] *How Religious are Americans?*, GALLUP (March 29, 2024), https://news.gallup.com/poll/358364/religious-americans.aspx.

[20] *More Americans pray in their car than in a place of worship*, SALT LAKE TRIBUNE (May 4, 2023), https://www.sltrib.com/religion/2023/05/04/more-americans-pray-their-car-than/.

A 2022 Gallup Poll report found that sixty-nine percent of Americans believe the Bible to be the "inspired word of God,"[21] though some take the Bible more literally than others.[22] Even among those who do *not* believe that the Bible is the "inspired word of God" are people who listen to Moses, the prophets, and Jesus because they believe them to be great moral leaders. What is common among all these people is that they, in some way, look to biblical teaching for moral guidance.[23]

Of course, the fact that people have religious beliefs and are active in religious organizations does not necessarily mean that their religious values affect the way they act in business dealings or in legal controversies. Religious belief is probably more likely to influence what Americans do in church, synagogue, mosque, and home than in the law office or corporate boardroom. However, it may be that people do not put their moral beliefs into practice in the law office and that moral directions taken in the law office are routinely self-serving, precisely because we do not talk about the moral and religious values that people bring to the law office.

If lawyers are to talk with clients about the moral values clients actually have, they may have to talk about religious moral beliefs. If they look, lawyers and clients will find that their religious sources have much to say about problems that arise in legal representation,[24] although, of course, even those who start with religious morality will not always find clear or easy answers. Biblical answers are sometimes clear, sometimes not. Biblical answers are sometimes easy, often not. Just as adherents of biblical morality come to different (often very different) positions on political and social issues,[25] they sometimes will reach different positions on issues that arise during legal representation. The important thing, we believe, is that they seek to locate, understand, and apply their values to these issues. Lawyers can help clients in this task. At the very least lawyers should not smother those values. In this book, we consider religious as well as secular moral values that might inform lawyers and clients in the law office.

---

[21] Frank Newport, *Fewer in U.S. Now See Bible as Literal Word of God*, GALLUP (July 6, 2022), *available at* https://news.gallup.com/poll/394262/fewer-bible-literal-word-god.aspx%E2%80%8C#:~:%E2%80%8Ctext=%E2%80%8CLine%20graph.,God%20to%20be%20taken%20literally.

[22] Twenty percent of those surveyed said that the Bible should always be interpreted literally; Forty-nine percent said it should not be interpreted literally in every instance. *Id.*

[23] "Over half of U.S. adults (54%) believe that America would be worse off without the Bible," whereas only 14% believe America would be better off without the Bible. *State of the Bible 2021: Five Key Findings*, BARNA (May 19, 2021), https://www.barna.com/research/sotb-2021/.

[24] See, e.g., the section entitled "Counselling Christian Clients" in Robert F. Cochran Jr., The Servant Lawyer: Facing the Challenges of Christian Faith in Everyday Law Practice 143–151 (InterVarsity Press Academic, 2024).

[25] *See* James Davison Hunter, The Culture Wars 88 (1991); Frank Newport, *The Politics of Religion* (Sept. 1, 2023), https://news.gallup.com/opinion/polling-matters/510464/politics-religion.aspx.

4. MORAL VALUES FOR THE LAW OFFICE

Moral problems touching almost every area of life arise in legal representation. Should a hospital "pull the plug" on a comatose patient? Should a husband leave his wife and children? Should a company give drug tests to employees? Should it move its factory overseas and lay off its workers in this country? Clients and lawyers who are concerned with morality in the law office wrestle with all sorts of moral issues. Lawyers who specialize (family law, health care law, labor law, corporate law, taxation, landlord-tenant law, etc.) will have special moral issues that accompany their specialties.

We propose to look at three moral considerations that seem to arise throughout legal practice: justice, mercy, and truthfulness. It does not require a degree in philosophy or theology to recognize them. They are part of the stories we learned as children. They are part of the religious and moral values of people in almost all cultures, and we believe that there is an intuitive attraction to each of them that is likely to influence clients and lawyers.

That is not to suggest that moral judgment following or using these values is simple. Anyone who has tried to be just, merciful, and truthful knows that. Different principles or virtues, and sometimes the same principle or virtue, may support different assessments of a situation. It could be that the moral life is more about how we approach situations than the rules we discern for them.

CHAPTER 7

JUSTICE

■ ■ ■

Justice has been at the heart of morality in many cultures, including those of the early Greeks and Hebrews and today's descendants of the Enlightenment. However, different traditions have different concepts of justice.[1] Aristotle recognized two types of justice: corrective justice—placing the parties where they were before one wronged the other—and distributive justice—the just distribution of goods within a society.[2] In the last two centuries, the concept of social justice has engulfed the concept of distributive justice, concerning itself with social and political welfare as well as with the distribution of economic goods. According to Aristotle, justice is both a virtue to be exercised by citizens and a responsibility of the state—it belongs in the law office and in the legislature and courthouse. He contrasts the virtue of justice with the vice of acquisitiveness.[3] (This may explain the tendency of some to exclude discussions of justice from the law office—recall that Dr. Robert S. Redmount identified acquisitiveness as a characteristic of many lawyers which they impute to their clients.[4]) Two additional notions of justice concern criminal cases—retributive justice and restorative justice. This chapter will explore how all these forms of justice might come into play in the lives of lawyers and clients.

1. A STORY OF CORRECTIVE JUSTICE: THE BROKER'S COMMISSION

We turn first to a law office story that raises a corrective justice concern.[5]

* * *

Dr. Robert Bartle, a dentist, opened his office last year for the practice of dentistry in West View, a prosperous suburban neighborhood. Although he had not initially planned to do so, he

---

1 As Alasdair MacIntyre has pointed out in his book, Whose Justice? Which Rationality? (1988), different traditions have different concepts of rationality, which yield different concepts of justice.

2 *See* Aristotle, Nicomachean Ethics, chs. 2–4 (Oswald trans., 1962). For a further discussion of Aristotle's concept of corrective justice, *see infra* this Chapter, Section One.

3 MacIntyre, *supra* Chapter 7 note 1, at 111.

4 *See supra* text accompanying Chapter 1 note 9.

5 This story is adapted from a lecture by the late Louis M. Brown.

bought the building in which he has his office after a survey of rental offices and after learning that rents for offices were much higher than he anticipated.

When he decided to look for a building to buy, he consulted a real estate broker named Annie Skagg, whose office is also in West View. She had listed a small, unoccupied, two-story building in a desirable commercial neighborhood, the second floor of which was ideal for Dr. Bartle's needs. He bought the building through her agency and was satisfied with her services.

Dr. Bartle did not use the ground floor, but the ground floor was soon occupied. Two weeks after he moved in, he was approached by one William Cody, who was looking for premises in which to open a tackle shop. He said he had learned about Dr. Bartle's building from Annie Skagg. After a day or two of negotiation between Mr. Cody and Dr. Bartle, the two agreed on rent and on lease terms and Mr. Cody became Dr. Bartle's tenant. Tenant and landlord have since then dealt with one another cordially.

Last week, Dr. Bartle received a bill for a rental real-estate commission from Ms. Skagg's office. The bill was for the customary local rental commission; it came to just under $3,000. Dr. Bartle consulted Jaime Jaramillo, a lawyer. After initial courtesies, their conversation was as follows:

Jaramillo: Have you had any prior dealings with Ms. Skaggs's agency? I mean, other than the purchase of your building?

Bartle: No. Only in the purchase of my property.

Jaramillo: And you had no written agreement with anybody in her office concerning the rental arrangement with Cody—only her request for this money, after the fact?

Bartle: Yes. That's right. She didn't say anything about getting a commission until after Cody was in and in operation. As far as I am concerned, I shouldn't have to pay her anything. I don't know if I really have to. However, I assume I do. I don't know. Do I have an obligation to pay?

Jaramillo: Under our law, any arrangement or agreement between you and a broker, which is not written down, is unenforceable. It is in our statute of frauds.

Bartle: Frauds?

Jaramillo: Yes. But that doesn't mean there has to be a fraud involved. It's an old title for the statute—goes back to England, I think. The idea is that the statute *prevents* frauds by requiring some contracts to be in writing. Otherwise they cannot be enforced.

Bartle: Well, I don't think there is any *fraud* here. I don't think Annie Skaggs is trying to defraud anybody, and I am certainly not.

Jaramillo: Of course not.

Bartle: But, under this law, I could just tell her good-bye and leave me alone?

Jaramillo: There is nothing she could do about it.

Bartle: Maybe that is just what I will do. I will say my lawyer told me.

Jaramillo: But, I think also you have some extra-legal considerations that you shouldn't lose sight of—in terms of your business reputation, I mean, your reputation in the West View business community. In terms, too, of whether you are ever going to have dealings with Ms. Skaggs's office or any other real-estate brokers there.

Bartle: What are you telling me then? That I should pay her or that I shouldn't?

Jaramillo: I'm not telling you that you should pay her or not pay her, but I think, in making your decision, you have to consider not just your legal obligations, but also other considerations. It is up to you to decide how significant these obligations are to you. You see, we don't know how difficult it would have been for you to get somebody to become a tenant in that building. And, after all, she did get somebody in there for you. Cody is now paying you for the rental. You're getting money out of it that you might not have if Ms. Skaggs had not sent Cody to you. So you're getting a benefit conferred on you right now.

Bartle: That's true.

Jaramillo: It is also true that you may not technically be liable to her, and I am not saying that it shouldn't be an important consideration. Obviously it is. We might need to talk about what would be a fair commission, if you decide she should get a commission.

Bartle: Well, all right. Thank you for your advice. I suppose I have to pay her.

* * *

Before we look at the concept of justice that is discussed between Dr. Bartle and Jaramillo, note a few other things about their conversation. First, the problem the parties faced is a common one in the law office. Clients often can obtain a legal result that is inconsistent with justice. The law may preclude a just claim for the sake of other legal values. The statute of frauds, the statute at issue in this case, encourages parties to establish written evidence of contract terms by precluding enforcement of some contracts that are not in writing. Another example is the statute of limitations, which encourages plaintiffs to bring claims in a timely manner by precluding claims brought after a certain period. And, with the rising cost of litigation, the most common legal way of avoiding a just claim is to say "So sue me" to an opposing party who is unlikely to have the resources to litigate.

In other cases, the client may be able to act unjustly because the law does not regulate the client's activity. The law may allow some types of racial discrimination (as it did, in 1961, in the segregated factories case), or allow a parent to pay very little child support. In other cases, the opposing party may be unable to obtain justice because he or she is unrepresented or poorly represented and may not be aware of what the law allows. Or, the client may be aware of facts, unknown to the other party, that show the client's claim to be unjust.

Note also how Dr. Bartle at first thinks he might avoid responsibility. Almost like a child testing a parent's tolerance, he makes a bid for his lawyer's approval ("Maybe that is just what I will do"). Then he tries to place moral responsibility on the lawyer ("I will say my lawyer told me"). Dr. Bartle wants to accept the benefits of the law, but his discomfort with that solution is evident—he wants to place blame as well as responsibility on his lawyer. This illustrates how easy it is for the lawyer's role to become one of not only telling clients of their rights, but serving as a justification for their assertion of those rights.

In this case, Jaramillo says that he is not telling his client to accept (or not accept) the benefits of the law. He shows respect for the conscience of his client, but as he does so he points to the benefit Dr. Bartle has received from the real estate agent's efforts. Jaramillo treats the interests of others seriously; at the end, so does his client. Maybe, in fact, Dr. Bartle had this concern for others all along. Maybe he needed a lawyer who would help him follow his better instincts.

The argument Jaramillo makes is a moral argument founded in the virtue of justice. He uses, as we lawyers often do, a phrase from law school—"benefit conferred"—to express his argument. That phrase comes from the early development of the law of restitution; it comes from the realization that the application of the common law of contracts might apply, not just in cases where there is a "meeting of the minds," but in cases in which the demanding party had done something valuable for the resisting party. Jaramillo is using it here, not to refer to the law, but to the business practices of a good person and the business custom in their community.

Aristotle said:

> Justice is that quality in terms of which we can say of a just person that he practices by choice what is just, and that, in making distribution between himself and another . . . he will not give himself the larger and his neighbor the smaller share of what is desirable . . . but he will give an equal share as determined by proportion. . . . Injustice . . . violates proportion.[6]

Jaramillo, in making his argument, appeals to what he assumes or trusts or hopes to be Dr. Bartle's practice of this virtue (or good habit) of justice. As it turns out, his assumption or trust or hope is well founded; the appeal works.

How does a lawyer raise the issue of justice with a client? In the real estate commission story, Jaramillo raises the moral issue by saying, "In making your decision, you have to consider not just your legal obligations, but also other considerations." He then describes the benefit that Dr. Bartle has received as a result of the real estate agent's efforts. "[O]ther considerations" is a somewhat vague way of referring to morality. Jaramillo seems to feel that justice in the law office is a matter that should be handled with some delicacy: If a lawyer raises the issue too strongly, the client may leave. Some clients don't like to be preached at. Jaramillo's lesson for other lawyers is that they should raise the issue in a way that will invite the client to think about it, to engage in moral discourse. Jaramillo makes his point, but maybe he stumbles into it. In the end, even with Jaramillo's emphasis on the decision being up to the client, it is not entirely clear that the client has been involved in the decision-making process. Dr. Bartle concludes the session with, "Well, all right . . . I suppose I have to pay her." We suppose he did pay her.

It also appears that Jaramillo sought to avoid the danger he would impose his view of justice on the client. The client should be able to participate fully in the decision and experience the moral development we feel is an important part of the attorney-client relationship (or the autonomy that others feel is at the heart of it). Lawyers must be careful not just to announce their perception of justice. (Lawyers often have

[6] Aristotle, *supra* Chapter 7 note 2.

enough power to impose their moral perceptions.) The client must be an active participant. Why? Because we believe that the lawyer's concern is not just that the client do the right thing but that the client be, become, continue to be, a good person.

We also believe the lawyer should participate in the discussion about what would be fair, as Jaramillo did when he pointed out the "benefit conferred" on his client and the work of the real estate agent. As we suggested in Chapter Five, the lawyer can introduce justice to the lawyer-client conversation, without imposing the lawyer's values on the client, by asking the client what would be fair.

A final thing to note from this story is that the real estate agent ultimately received a fee from Dr. Bartle. Some might suggest that if you want justice, you go to court. To assume that court is the place where people find justice is to assume that justice is something the state gives to people. More often, we suspect, justice is something people give to one another. Aristotle saw justice first as a personal virtue: "Justice is that quality in terms of which we can say of a just person that he practices by choice what is just." We suspect that justice is most likely to emerge if lawyers and clients on both sides seek it than if they rely upon the state to provide it.

2. DISTRIBUTIVE JUSTICE, SOCIAL JUSTICE, AND THE LAW OFFICE

Distributive and social justice have been subjects of concern of many of the great thinkers over the ages. Aristotle argued that distribution of goods should be based on desert, in proportion to the contribution that one makes to a society, but he acknowledged that what is considered deserving varies among different societies.[7]

Torah (a word that means both the first five books of the Bible and the whole of Jewish law) required that farmers leave a portion of their crops unharvested so the poor might gather them, that land be returned to the families that originally owned it every 50 years, and that debts be forgiven every seven years.[8] The Hebrew prophets measured the justice of a society by the way it cared for those who have no power: the widow, the orphan, and the alien.[9] Jews and Christians who draw their moral values from the Hebrew Scriptures rightly wrestle with the modern implications of the Torah and the prophets on the condition of the poor.

---

7 Aristotle, *supra* Chapter 7 note 2, ch. 5.

8 Deuteronomy 14:29, 24:17, 27:19.

9 The Hebrew concept of justice is closely related to the Hebrew concept of mercy, and we reserve a further discussion of it for the following chapter. *See infra* Chapter 8, Section 4.

John Stuart Mill identified the aim of social justice: "Society should treat all equally well who have deserved equally well of it. . ."[10]

Pope Pius XI argued that as a matter of social justice every person must take seriously the responsibility to order or reorganize his or her life in consideration of the common good.[11] The work of social justice aims at the good of all members of the community.

Social justice says to a lawyer that following the law, even following the law carefully and seeing to it that one's clients follow the law carefully, is not enough. Lawyers' understanding of social justice accounts for the creation of courts of equity in the Middle Ages. It also accounts for lawyers' common sense advice, "Be fair." And in the lives of clients who are communities—businesses, clubs, governments, religious congregations—the notion that the law is not enough shows up when these communities recognize the obvious and melancholy fact that they neglect some of their members, exploit them, harm them, and leave them behind. The history of religious movements for social justice, including modern Jewish prophets such as Louis D. Brandeis, the Social Gospel Movement among American Protestants, and encyclicals on social justice from modern leaders of the Catholic Church, often have been protests against the harm caused by apparently well-meaning and satisfied human communities.

Social justice in the practice of law is about caring for those who are neglected, exploited, harmed, and left behind by lawyers and the communities lawyers advise and represent. "The effective delivery of scarce legal goods . . . requires more than the provision of equal access, case-by-case representation, and zealous advocacy," as Anthony V. Alfieri put it, more, that is, than service *pro bono publico*. "Scarcity requires that effective legal change be measured not by the outcomes of individual cases, but rather by the progress of social change."[12] Social change can be contemplated and measured in law offices as much as in courts and legislatures. Social justice requires sacrifice on the part of those who have wealth and power. The rabbinical "Ethics of the Fathers" put it this way: "He who says, What is mine is mine and what is thine is thine, that man speaks like a citizen of Sodom."[13]

---

[10] *Quoted in* Michael Novak, *Defining Social Justice*, First Things, Dec. 2000, at 11, 12.

[11] *See* William J. Ferree, Introduction to Social Justice (1948) 41–42.

[12] Anthony V. Alfieri, *(Un)covering Identity in Civil Rights and Poverty Law*, 121 HARV. L. REV. 805, 806 (2008). Note that when it amended Standard 303(b)(3), the ABA also added Standard 303(c) which focuses on providing opportunities for students to learn about bias, cultural competence and racism. "A law school shall provide education to law students on bias, cross-cultural competency, and racism: (1) at the start of the program of legal education, and (2) at least once again before graduation." STANDARDS & RULES OF PROC. FOR APPROVAL OF LAW SCHOOLS, Standard 303(c) (Am. Bar Ass'n. Section of Leg. Educ. & Admissions to the Bar 2024–25).

[13] Ethics of the Fathers, V, 13, *quoted in* The Pentateuch and Haftorahs 929 (J. H. Hertz ed., 2nd ed. 1987).

Social justice, then, seeks to apply broader moral judgment—beyond distributive justice and procedural justice. It has been reflected in political and legal movements, through the work of lawyers in the United States, from the concept of "person" in the Bill of Rights, to freeing slaves, to the emancipation of women, to the modern Civil Rights Movement (centrally a movement of lawyers, by the way). One way to look at the issue is to notice that social justice can be said to dig deeper for what is due the human person. The human person is something more, something deeper, than just a citizen or a party in a lawsuit. James Wilson, one of the founding members of the United States Supreme Court, noticed this and wrote in an early judicial opinion that perhaps the American state—the law—might well be called "the noblest work of Man." "But," he said, Man is "the noblest work of God."[14]

Concerns with social justice can arise at several places in the work of a lawyer. First, lawyers might directly serve the poor and disadvantaged by representing them, either as legal aid or pro bono attorneys. There is a special reward that comes with such work: that look of surprise and gratitude in the eyes of clients—someone is finally listening to them, paying attention to their problems, trying to get them some relief. We hope all lawyers receive that blessing.

Lawyers can also assist the poor and the broader community by engaging in law reform. Lawyers see law on a day-to-day basis. They see where it works and where it does not work. Lawyers are trained to "think like lawyers"—to recognize problems and figure out solutions. They can propose changes in the law to legislatures, administrative agencies, and city councils.

Finally, we hope lawyers do not miss the opportunity to serve the poor in the full range of types of practice. If helping the poor is the objective, we are not sure whether it is best to work in a legal aid office or a large corporate firm. As Robert E. Rodes, Jr., has argued to his students:

> The burdens of the poor are being fashioned in corporate law offices downtown faster than they can be relieved by the legal aid offices or by the government. Lawyers who advocate the cause of the poor before their business clients will probably do the poor at least as much good as lawyers who represent them in court. Lawyers can exercise a preferential option for the poor in any kind of practice.[15]

---

[14] *Chisholm v. Georgia, supra* Introduction note 3, at 462–63.

[15] Robert E. Rodes, Jr., Pilgrim Law 105 (1998).

3. ATTORNEY BRANDEIS AND SOCIAL JUSTICE

There is much that could be said about Louis D. Brandeis. He went to Harvard Law School straight out of high school and attained the highest marks ever earned. He founded one of the country's leading law firms. He invented the "Brandeis Brief" (his brief in the *Muller* case had two pages of legal argument and over 100 pages of sociological evidence). Chief Justice Horace Gray of the Massachusetts Supreme Court, later a justice on the United States Supreme Court, said that Brandeis was "the most ingenious and most original lawyer I ever met."[16] As a United States Supreme Court Justice, Brandeis wrote groundbreaking opinions in support of free speech and press, privacy, and judicial restraint. President Franklin D. Roosevelt saw him as a prophet, calling him "Isaiah," though Brandeis played a key role in killing Roosevelt's Court-packing proposal.[17] Justice Harlan Fiske Stone identified Brandeis's key characteristics as "social conscience and vision, infinite patience, an extraordinary capacity for sustained intellectual effort, and serene confidence that truth revealed will ultimately prevail."[18]

We want to focus on Brandeis the lawyer. He practiced law for almost 40 years before he joined the Supreme Court. We want to hold up Brandeis the lawyer as a model of the many ways a lawyer can be a proponent of social justice in the midst of an active law career—representing the poor and the public interest on a *pro bono* basis, advocating thoughtful law reform, and representing wealthy and powerful clients in a way that takes into consideration the interests of all who are affected by what these clients do with their wealth and power.

Public Interest Advocate. Brandeis worked to protect the public interest, earning the title, "The People's Lawyer." During most of the period that he practiced law, his life was full of activities on behalf of the public: writing law review articles, testifying before legislative committees, giving speeches to public interest organizations, trying cases, and writing briefs on behalf of the public interest. He and his law partner wrote *the* article on the then novel invasion of privacy tort, an article William Prosser later identified as the most influential law review article ever written.[19] Brandeis was an early advocate for many social programs that we today take for granted: antitrust legislation, industrial safety laws, wage and hour regulation, workers' compensation, public health, public

---

[16] Lewis J. Paper, Brandeis: An Intimate Biography of One of America's Truly Great Supreme Court Justices 24–25 (1983), *quoting* Alpheus Thomas Mason, Brandeis: A Free Man's Life 61 (1946).

[17] *Id.* at 2.

[18] Tribute at 1942 meeting of the Court to honor Brandeis, *quoted in* Stephen W. Baskerville, Of Laws and Limitations: An Intellectual Portrait of Louis Dembitz Brandeis 233 (1994).

[19] *See, e.g.,* William Prosser, *Privacy,* 48 CAL. L. REV. 383 (1960).

transportation, conservation, utility rate adjustments, life insurance regulation, and urban planning.

Brandeis refused payment for his public interest cases. Earnings from his corporate practice financed them. Not wanting to be a burden to his law partners, he paid his firm "for the privilege of using his time for public service." He paid his firm $25,000 for the work he did in one public interest case.[20] When asked about his sacrifice, Brandeis responded:

> Some men buy diamonds and rare works of art; others delight in automobiles and yachts. My luxury is to invest my surplus effort, beyond that required for the proper support of my family, to the pleasure of taking up a problem and solving, or helping to solve it, for the people without receiving any compensation.[21]

Shortly after Brandeis was confirmed to be an associate justice on the Supreme Court, a Boston legal activist wrote in a letter to Brandeis that he was more sorry than glad at Brandeis's appointment. "As long as you were in private life, it seemed to me that, if any monstrous injustice should be attempted upon helpless people, they would not lack protection."[22]

A "Judicial Attitude Toward His Clients." Brandeis's efforts for the public extended beyond his *pro bono* practice to his corporate practice. Brandeis refused to advocate causes that he considered to be unjust and he counseled his clients to act in a just manner. We might not know about these aspects of his practice but for the fact that they were used against him in the Senate confirmation hearings following his appointment to the Court. "A banker testified that Brandeis, as a lawyer, had required satisfaction of the justness of the banker's cause before deciding to take it on. No other lawyer he had ever dealt with, the banker testified, raised that question."[23] Austen Fox testified that: "The trouble with Mr. Brandeis is that he never loses his judicial attitude toward his clients. He always acts the part of a judge toward his clients instead of being his clients' lawyer, which is against the practices of the bar."[24] (Maybe it is not surprising that

---

[20] *See* Thomas L. Shaffer, American Legal Ethics 242 (1985). *citing* Albert Vorspan, Giants of Justice (1960).

[21] *Id.* at 243 *and* Michael Schudson, *Public, Private and Professional Lives: The Correspondence of David Dudley Field and Samuel Bowles*, 21 AM. J. LEGAL HIST. 191, 211 (1977).

[22] Letter from Amos Pinchot to Louis D. Brandeis (June 6, 1916), *in* 4 Letters of Louis D. Brandeis, 239–40 (Melvin I. Urofsky & David W. Levy eds., 1971), *quoted in* Paper, *supra* Chapter 7 note 16, at 242.

[23] Shaffer, *supra* Chapter 7 note 20, at 242, *quoting* Schudson, *supra* Chapter 7 note 21, at 210. For further discussion of Brandeis and his law practice, *see* Shaffer, *supra* Chapter 7 note 20, at 241–314 and Robert F. Cochran, Jr., *Louis D. Brandeis and the Lawyer Advocacy System*, in "Symposium: The Lawyer of the Future," 39 PEPP. L.REV. 351 (2013).

[24] *Quoted in* Shaffer, *supra* Chapter 7 note 20, at 242. We acknowledge that Brandeis' counsel of his wealthy and powerful clients might have been more that of a Guru than a Friend. But, as we argued in Chapter Four, Part Eight, friends may need to be more assertive with powerful friends than weak friends. In order for moral discourse to be effective, lawyers may need to be more assertive with powerful clients who have the potential to cause greater harm to other people and are unlikely to be overwhelmed by the lawyer's moral counsel.

Brandeis was ultimately confirmed. With enemies like that who needs friends?)

Practical Wisdom. Brandeis applied the great lawyer virtue of practical wisdom to the issues he addressed, whether they concerned a client's business or the great social issues of his day. He combined his concern for all the people who might be affected by his and his clients' actions with his famous creativity and attention to detail. These qualities in many cases enabled him to come up with a solution that worked to the benefit of all.

In one case, for example, shoe manufacturer W.H. McElwain hired Brandeis to negotiate a cut in the hours of his employees, in light of the economic stresses the business faced. Instead, Brandeis figured out a means of restructuring the client's business that allowed the workers to work longer hours and the company to make more money.[25] "Brandeis urged lawyers to try to steer people away from wasteful squabbling and to craft new frameworks of mutually beneficial collaboration. This required lawyers to go beyond the law and understand the client's practical circumstances."[26]

Brandeis's concern for all the parties extended to his public interest advocacy as well. At times, he generated the enmity of both sides of disputes. Big business interests aggressively opposed his confirmation to the Supreme Court, but many on the labor side believed that Brandeis's proposals did not sufficiently benefit their cause. For his failure to support all of labor's demands, Wobblies' leader "Big Bill" Haywood called him "the most dangerous man in the United States."[27] Part of his "danger" was that workers had grown to trust him. Brandeis was probably so successful because his proposals recognized the broad range of interests that were involved.

"The Opportunity in the Law." We conclude this section on social justice with Brandeis's own comments about the practice of law. Though presented to law students over 100 years ago, his comments seem uncomfortably current and present a worthy challenge to those of us in and entering the legal profession today:

> [A]t the present time the lawyer does not hold as high a position with the people as he held [previously]; but the reason is not lack of opportunity. It is this: Instead of holding a position of independence, between the wealthy and the people, prepared to curb the excesses of either, able lawyers have, to a large extent, allowed themselves to become adjuncts of great corporations and have neglected the obligation to use their powers for the

[25] Melvin I. Urofsky, Louis D. Brandeis and the Progressive Tradition 8 (1981).

[26] Paper, *supra* Chapter 7 note 16, at 64–65.

[27] *Quoted in* Baskerville, *supra* Chapter 7 note 18, at 156.

> protection of the people. We hear much of the "corporation lawyer," and far too little of the "people's lawyer." The great opportunity of the American Bar is and will be to stand again as it did in the past, ready to protect also the interests of the people.
>
> . . .
>
> Here, consequently, is the great opportunity in the law. The next generation must witness a continuing and ever-increasing contest between those who have and those who have not. . . . The people are beginning to doubt whether . . . there is a justification for the great inequalities in the distribution of wealth, for the rapid creation of fortunes, more mysterious than the deeds of Aladdin's lamp. . . . The people's thought will take shape in action; and it lies with us, with you to whom in part the future belongs, to say on what lines the action is to be expressed; whether it is to be expressed wisely and temperately, or wildly and intemperately; whether it is to be expressed on lines of evolution or on lines of revolution. Nothing can better fit you for taking part in the solution of these problems, than the study and preeminently the practice of law. Those of you who feel drawn to that profession may rest assured that you will find in it an opportunity for usefulness which is probably unequaled. There is a call upon the legal profession to do a great work for this country.[28]

4. CONCEPTS OF JUSTICE AND THE LAW OFFICE

John Rawls, coming out of the Enlightenment and liberalism's focus on individual preference and reason, does not define justice; he creates a procedure for identifying justice: Justice is that situation which rational people would agree to if they stood behind a veil of ignorance about their circumstances, *i.e.*, they did not know whether the result would profit them or not.[29]

A lawyer might bring Rawls's concept to the law office. A lawyer could tell a client to imagine that he or she was approaching a legal problem "behind a veil of ignorance," not knowing whether he or she would be the plaintiff or defendant (in litigation) or the party of the first or second part (in contract negotiation), and then to determine the just result. However, we think that such an abstract exercise would be unlikely to be helpful.

The people who stand behind Rawls's veil of ignorance are those who are viewed as the ideal by proponents of liberal democracy: the rational, the independent, the autonomous. They (in theory) leave behind any

---

[28] Louis D. Brandeis, *The Opportunity in the Law*, in Business: A Profession 313, 321–27 (1914).

[29] *See* John Rawls, A Theory of Justice (1971).

affiliation they have which is based on characteristics they do not share with all persons.[30] As Martha Minow has suggested:

> Underlying [Rawls's] theory is the idea of the abstract individual. This individual is thought to have wants, desires, and needs independent of social context, relationships with others, or historical setting. The individual, in short, is distinguishable from his or her situation and social, political, and religious identities. . . .[31]

We do not think such a person exists, nor that it is a helpful exercise to imagine what such a person would do. We think lawyers are more helpful to clients in identifying justice if they help clients to apply the concepts of justice clients gain from their family, community, church, and synagogue—the sources of insight Rawls asks the lonely individual to leave behind.

Moral psychologist Lawrence Kohlberg, who also approaches the question of justice from the perspective of liberal democracy, argues that the concept of justice encompasses all of morality.[32] For Kohlberg, morality is protecting the rights of others. He identifies three levels of moral development. At the preconventional level, people are moral because of a fear of punishment and because morality serves their interests. At the conventional level, morality is based on the preservation of relationships and obedience to agreed-upon rules and assumed duties. At the postconventional level, people uphold basic rights and values, even when they conflict with or go beyond the rules contained in lower levels.[33]

We can illustrate Kohlberg's levels of moral reasoning if we look again at the segregated factories story (Chapter Three). Assuming that integration would have worked to the disadvantage of the company (because of social disruption, etc.), a company official who operated solely at the preconventional level would have integrated the factories only if it appeared that the law required integration and that the company would have suffered a substantial penalty for failure to comply. A company official who operated at the conventional level would have integrated if the law or local custom required integration (even if the law was not enforced or the penalty for a violation was quite small). And a company official who operated at the postconventional level would have integrated, whether or not the law required the company to do so, because it would uphold a basic right of people not to be discriminated against.

---

[30] *See* Michael Sandel, Liberalism and the Limits of Justice (1982), *cited in* Martha Minow, Making All the Difference: Inclusion, Exclusion, and American Law 151 (1990).

[31] Minow, *supra* Chapter 7 note 30, at 151–52.

[32] Lawrence Kohlberg, Essays on Moral Development: The Philosophy of Moral Development 30–31 (1981).

[33] *See id.* at 409–12 (Kohlberg identifies two stages within each level).

If we follow Kohlberg's framework, lawyers can address clients at any of the three levels of moral reasoning. At the preconventional level, lawyers can explain to clients the costs of various options to them: "If you shoplift again, the judge will send you to jail." "If you do not settle, you will spend more on attorney's fees than you can expect to gain at trial." At the conventional level, lawyers can warn clients of the risks that their actions will create to their relationships and remind them of their contractual and civic duties: "A suit will destroy your relationship with your daughter and son-in-law." "He is unlikely to enforce the agreement, but you agreed to repay the loan." At the postconventional level lawyers can invite clients to uphold basic rights and values, even when they depart from the law or from agreed-upon rules and duties: "You are not required to integrate, but what do you think would be the right thing to do?" "This sit-in demonstration will violate trespass laws, but it might help to combat racial discrimination." All of these levels of moral conversation have to do with justice.

Lawyers probably operate with clients most often at Kohlberg's first two levels, the preconventional level (they inform clients of the dictates of the law and the penalties they are likely to incur if they disobey) and the conventional level (they discuss with clients the requirements of the law, of custom, and of their contractual responsibilities). Both we and the admonitions of our professional codes advocate that lawyers go beyond the preconventional and conventional and talk with clients about what would be fair. Lawyers are often in a position to enable their clients to see moral issues in terms of the higher stages of justice.[34]

5. LAWYERS AND THE TRADITIONAL CRIMINAL JUSTICE SYSTEM

Previous sections of this chapter have focused on lawyers, clients, and justice in civil cases. Of course, justice concerns arise in criminal cases as well. In the United States, the federal government, as well as many state governments, label the departments responsible for prosecuting crimes "justice" departments. The work of both prosecuting attorneys and criminal defense lawyers is much concerned with justice. But the criminal justice system is concerned with factors in addition to justice. It strikes a balance between truth, justice, and defendant rights and the arguments of prosecutors and defense attorneys help judges and juries make wise choices as to that balance.

The Goals of the Criminal Justice System. On the first day of Criminal Law class, countless law professors around the world ask students to identify the purposes of criminal law. Which are appropriate? Can they be

---

[34] Darcia Narvaez makes this suggestion for counselors. Narvaez, *Counseling for Morality: A Look at the Four-Component Model,* 10 J. OF PSYCH. AND CHRISTIANITY 358, 361 (1991).

reconciled with one another? Students (and criminal law textbook authors) supply several possible answers—retributive justice, deterrence, incapacitation, and rehabilitation. In many respects, these goals reinforce one another, but in other respects, they are in tension.

Retributive justice suggests that the punishment should fit the crime. "An eye for an eye." Guilty defendants should pay their due to society based on the harm they intended and the harm they inflicted. The state should punish them because they deserve it. As Jean Hampton has suggested, such punishment affirms the worth of the victim. Implicit in a defendant's crime is generally an assertion that he or she is of greater value than the victim. The imposition of retributive punishment says this is not true. The victim deserves respect. Imposing a punishment that fits the crime asserts that the victim is of equal value to the defendant.[35] By imposing retributive punishment, the government asserts both that the victim has value and that what the defendant did was wrong.

In addition, the hope is that criminal punishment will deter future crime, both by the defendant and by the public. Defendants directly experience punishment and (hopefully) will shun crime in the future. Moreover, imprisonment incapacitates some criminals for a time. Punishment of defendants also deters both victims and the broader population from committing crime. If the government punishes guilty defendants, victims are less likely to seek personal revenge and the fear of punishment will deter people from committing crimes.

There is also a hope that the time criminals spend in prison—time in "correctional facilities"—might be an occasion for rehabilitation—that prisoners will learn skills that will enable them to get jobs and live productive lives upon their release.

In many respects, however, the criminal justice system falls short of its goals. Criminal punishment is often haphazard, with vastly different punishments for the same crime. Persons of color and poor people receive harsher penalties than their white and wealthy counterparts. Punishment seems arbitrary, encouraging disobedience, rather than obedience to law. Law fails to be a moral teacher. Many aspects of prison push prisoners toward, rather than away from, a life of crime. Prisoners separate into gangs for their own protection. Rape is common. Prisoners leave the legal system resentful and angry. Many come out hardened, educated in criminal techniques, with new friends who are likely to lead them astray. And defendants are not the only recipients of punishment. Punishment of a parent invariably affects the rest of the family. Prisoners' children are

---

[35] *See* Jeffrie G. Murphy & Jean Hampton, Forgiveness and Mercy (United Kingdom: Cambridge University Press, 1988), 124–28 (section by Jean Hampton), excerpted in Joshua Dressler & Stephen P. Garvey, Criminal Law: Cases and Materials, 7th ed. (St. Paul, MN: West Academic Publishing, 2016), 49–50.

often separated from their parents during crucial times of childhood development.

The criminal justice system presents both opportunities and challenges to prosecutors and defense attorneys.

Prosecutors. Most trial lawyers pursue justice indirectly. They advocate client interests as part of an adversary system that seeks justice. The hope is that among conflicting voices, judges and juries will identify truth and justice. Prosecutors serve as advocates in that system, but the legal system also requires them to seek justice directly. As the U. S. Supreme Court has said, the prosecutor represents the government, whose obligation "in a criminal prosecution is not that it shall win a case, but that justice shall be done."[36] Prosecutors should not merely be advocates on behalf of the state; they should determine what is just and pursue it. However, determining justice is complex. Prosecutors should consider many factors when determining the demands of justice in an individual case.

The prosecutor's role is daunting because they have such great power. In some respects, their power is greater than that of the judge. Prosecutors generally determine whether a case will be brought. A judge will not even see a case unless a prosecutor brings charges. Moreover, merely bringing a case can destroy a defendant. Prosecutors can charge defendants with multiple crimes for a single offense, compounding potential punishment and giving defendants little alternative but to plead guilty, whether they are guilty or not.

Fortunately, there are some checks on a prosecutor's power. The criminal justice system, like the civil justice system, is an adversary system. The defense attorney, as well as the judge and the jury, serve as checks on the prosecutor, though the "justice" system continues to convict a high number of innocent defendants.[37]

Criminal Defense. Criminal defense attorneys make sure prosecutors prove each element of a crime beyond a reasonable doubt. They hold the prosecutor to his or her burden of proof and raise potential defenses. Generally, however, the prosecutor "has the goods" on the defendant. The prosecutor would not have brought a charge if he or she did not have sufficient evidence to obtain a conviction. In such cases, the defense attorney's most important job may be finding some basis for limiting the

---

[36] *Berger v. United States*, 295 US 78, 88 (1935). *See also* ABA Standards for the Prosecution Function § 3–1.2(c) (1992) ("The duty of the prosecutor is to seek justice, not merely convict"). For a history of this duty, *see* Bruce A. Green, *Why Should Prosecutors "Seek Justice"?*, 26 FORDHAM URB. L.J. 607 (1999).

[37] The National Registry of Exonerations, which documents that over 3600 people have been exonerated since 1989, suggests that the checks on prosecutors have not been sufficiently robust to avoid wrongful convictions. https://www.law.umich.edu/special/exoneration/Pages/about.aspx See also Innocence Project, https://innocenceproject.org/exonerations-data/.

client's sentence. That will require the defense attorney to learn about the defendant's background, identify explanations for the defendant's crime, interview the defendant's family members, check with psychologists, and find alternative placements. Unlike prosecutors, criminal defense attorneys represent individual clients. Throughout the process of representation, they should discuss important decisions with the client and generally defer to the client. The law specifically reserves some decisions for the criminal defense client.[38] Defense attorneys might serve in any of the counseling roles we discussed in Chapters One through Four of this book—Autocrat, Hired Gun, Guru, or Friend. We believe, as in other types of practice, that the lawyer should act as a friend to the client—raising moral issues for discussion, but deferring to the client for resolution.[39]

In addition to providing legal representation for clients, it may be that a defense lawyer can help clients avoid future criminal difficulties. The defense lawyer may be in a strategically important position for such a role. He or she is often the primary person with whom a defendant has a personal relationship during the representation. Some clients grow to respect their attorneys and attorneys may gain influence.

Los Angeles attorney La Shae Henderson serves as a helpful role model. She was inspired in her work by her brother's death in a police shooting while he was engaged in a gun store robbery. La Shae became a criminal defense attorney for indigent clients, representing many defendants who were on the same road traveled earlier by her brother. She gave them a careful defense, but when their cases were over, she encouraged them to take responsibility for their lives. She told them: "Now our job is to figure out how we can avoid this happening again." Here is how La Shae describes her counseling role with clients:

> When people come to the court system they are ashamed, fearful, and embarrassed to be there. My goal is to develop a rapport with each client and to build their trust. The client usually will share more when he or she feels more comfortable. This opens the opportunity to give counsel, wisdom, and legal advice. Such advice will usually go beyond courtroom issues and that is the opportunity to discuss personal growth, healing, life changes, and opens the door to taking responsibility and pursuing reconciliation and restoration.[40]

Not everyone has the standing or the inclination to be as direct as La Shae is with her clients. If such counsel is done poorly, defendants may

---

[38] *See* Model Rules of Prof. Conduct 1.2(a), *supra* Chapter 3 note 8 ("In a criminal case, the lawyer shall abide by the client's decision, after consultation with the lawyer, as to a plea to be entered, whether to waive jury trial and whether the client will testify.")

[39] *See* Robert F. Cochran, Jr., *Crime, Confession, and the Counselor-at-Law: Lessons From Dostoyevsky*, 35 HOUSTON L. REV. 327–97 (1998).

[40] Email to Robert Cochran from La Shae Henderson (on file with authors).

come to see their attorney as just another part of a system that is against them. However, a compassionate, wise attorney may influence clients to alter the trajectory of their lives. The defense attorney may become a real friend to the client.

Both prosecutors and defense attorneys play an important role in the system's ability to protect the public, deliver justice, and—in some cases—reform lives. We now consider an alternate form of criminal procedure that seeks to determine justice and restore victims, defendants, and communities.

6. RESTORATIVE JUSTICE

Restorative justice is emerging as an alternative to retributive justice in some communities. It seeks through involvement of all the people affected by a crime to find a solution that will enable victims, defendants, and the community to heal wounds and avoid future crimes. Prosecutors, defense attorneys, and defendants play very different roles under restorative justice practice than under the traditional system.

In the traditional justice system,[41] lawyers—the prosecutor, the defense attorney, and the judge—are in control. Prosecutors and defense attorneys plea bargain and fight in court. Whereas the prosecutor, defense attorney, judge, and jury are the primary players in the traditional system, in a restorative justice system, the primary players are the victim, the defendant, their families, and their communities.

In the traditional system, prosecutors, rather than victims, make prosecution decisions. There are strengths and weaknesses in the prosecutor's being in control. Victims are likely to have a deep emotional reaction to a crime and may have difficulty determining what should be done. Some victims will want to punish the defendant based on vindictive passions—anger, hatred, spite, malice, envy, and cruelty. Other victims may be subject to the defendant's coercive influence or may want to forgive the defendant, when the defendant needs to be deterred, punished, and restrained. Prosecutors and judges provide a level of objectivity about such decisions.

However, in the traditional system, victims and defendants—the people most affected by criminal cases—tend to get lost. They are almost completely passive. A group of strangers—prosecutor, defense attorney, judge, and jury—make decisions that will affect victims and defendants for the rest of their lives. Prosecutors are likely to focus on the needs of the public and on winning their cases and to treat victims primarily as sources

[41] Some restorative justice proponents argue that restorative justice *is* the "traditional justice system." It is rooted in religious and cultural practices that go back many centuries. However, we suspect most of our readers think of lawyers, judges, and juries in the adversary system as the traditional system and we will stick with that use of the term.

of information. Defense attorneys are likely to focus on winning their cases. They tend to isolate their clients, often telling clients not to talk to anyone about the case for fear clients will reveal damaging information.

An additional weakness of the traditional system is that the available remedies often fail to address and often exacerbate the underlying problems of crime. If a court finds a defendant guilty, generally, the court's primary option is to imprison the defendant, and, as we have noted, prison tends to generate more crime. Often, the system leaves victims wondering, "Why did the defendant do this terrible thing to me?" To the defendant, generally the victim is a vague abstraction. Both the victim and the defendant often come out of the legal system more alienated, more wounded, and more angry than when they went in.

Restorative Justice. In 1990, with the publication of Howard Zehr's pathbreaking book *Changing Lenses: A New Focus for Crime and Justice*, "restorative justice" emerged as an alternative to the traditional system.[42] Restorative justice supporters have found fellow travelers among religious and indigenous communities around the globe.

Attempts at restorative justice can occur at any stage of the criminal justice process, from before the prosecutor brings charges to after the defendant has been convicted and imprisoned. In restorative justice, the victim, the defendant and members of their communities meet in a restorative justice "circle" and seek to identify means of addressing the injustices the defendant has caused and the victim has suffered. Restorative justice requires defendants to take responsibility for the harm they caused and seeks to provide victims with some form of restitution. It seeks to restore defendants to their communities. If a case is still in process, the restorative justice circle may make a recommendation to the court concerning its resolution.

We can explore the elements of restorative justice through an examination of a homicide case that occurred in Florida. Some jurisdictions use restorative justice only in minor cases, but as this case illustrates, restorative justice can address the most serious crimes.

Conor McBride and his fiancée Ann Grosmaire had dated for three years.[43] After a 38-hour argument, Conor shot and killed Ann and turned himself in to the Tallahassee Police Department. Assistant District Attorney Jack Campbell charged Conor with first-degree murder. A prison chaplain suggested that the parties explore restorative justice. Florida law had no official recognition of restorative justice, but the parties—including

[42] Howard Zehr, Changing Lenses: A New Focus for Crime and Justice (United States: Herald Press, 1990).

[43] For a fuller description of the case, see Paul Tullis, *Forgiven*, NEW YORK TIMES, January 6, 2013, section MM, p. 28, available at http://www.nytimes.com/2013/01/06/magazine/can-forgiveness-play-a-role-in-criminal-justice.html. The information and quotations in the text are from this article.

Jack Campbell—organized a restorative justice circle under a state provision for a confidential plea-bargaining conference.

There are four elements of restorative justice.[44]

(1) Inclusion. A restorative justice process seeks to involve all the affected parties in resolving the case. The "affected parties" will vary from case to case. They typically include the defendant, the victim, their families, and representatives of their communities. In Conor's case, the circle included Conor's parents, his attorney, Ann's parents, their priest, a victims' advocate, Assistant District Attorney Campbell, and a restorative justice facilitator.

(2) Encounter. The affected parties meet and discuss the offense, the harms, and the potential responses. Typically, each person is given an opportunity to speak about the crime and its effects.

In Conor's case, Ann's mother described Ann's life in detail. The power of her description struck those who witnessed the encounter.

> "She did not spare [Conor] in any way the cost of what he did," [the facilitator] remembers. "There were no kid gloves, none. It was really, really tough. Way tougher than anything a judge could say."
>
> "It was excruciating to listen to them talk," Campbell [the prosecutor] says. . . . "It was as traumatic as anything I've ever listened to in my life."

Conor described his emotional stress at the time of the shooting, expressed his sorrow, and took full responsibility.

(3) Repair. In restorative justice, the circle seeks to identify means of repairing the harm to victims and preventing future harm. The defendant repairs the injury to the extent possible. The community may assist in this responsibility. Howard Zehr notes that restorative justice "recognizes the need for outside authorities and in some cases imposed outcomes, [but] it prefers collaborative and inclusive processes and outcomes that are agreed upon, rather than imposed."[45] Repair under restorative justice goes beyond the remedies that are available under criminal law. The only official remedy available to victims in the traditional system is to bring a separate torts suit against the defendant (though prosecutors and judges in the traditional system may require defendants to pay reparations to the victim as a part of a plea deal).

The hope is that the people in a restorative justice circle together can discover what justice means in their situation. Restorative justice can

[44] Dan Van Ness, Karen Heetderks Strong, Jonathan Derby, and L. Lynette Parker, Restoring Justice: An Introduction to Restorative Justice, 6th ed. (New York: Routledge, 2022), 41.

[45] Howard Zehr, The Little Book of Restorative Justice: Revised and Updated (United States: Good Books, 2015), 35, 36–37.

enable the parties to develop a creative and personalized response. For example, in an arson case in which the defendant was convicted of burning a church building, the circle agreed that the defendant would assist with the church's landscaping when he was released.[46]

In Conor's case, of course, it was impossible to provide reparations for the harm. Ann's mother told Conor that he would need "to do the good works of two people because Ann is not here to do hers."

Typically, courts and prosecutors do not completely turn over responsibility for a remedy to the restorative justice circle. In some cases, the participants make recommendations to the court or prosecutor.

In Conor's case, Ann's mother recommended that Conor serve five to fifteen years; her father, ten to fifteen; and Conor's parents ten to fifteen. Jack Campbell, the prosecutor, agreed to twenty years as a part of a plea deal.

(4) Cohesion. A final hope of restorative justice is that the community can come together and enable the victim and the defendant to become whole, contributing members of the community. The participants in the restorative justice circle may identify means of addressing underlying causes of the harm that occurred. Studies indicate that defendants who participate in restorative justice processes are less likely to return to crime than those who experience only the traditional system.[47] It may be that a victim's story in the personal setting of a restorative justice circle is more likely to generate empathy in the defendant than it would in a traditional trial. In addition, it may be that defendants' participation in creating a plan for repair and restoration may make them more committed to carrying it through.

Attorneys and Restorative Justice. Decisions about whether to pursue restorative justice require wisdom on the part of parties and lawyers. In restorative justice, prosecutors and defense attorneys step back and give greater control to victims and defendants and the families and communities of each. But prosecutors and defense attorneys continue to have crucial roles—the prosecutor as representative of the public and the defense attorney as advisor to the defendant. The prosecutor ensures that the victim is protected in the process and that the process does not undercut the pedagogical and deterrent functions of the criminal law. The defense attorney ensures that defendants make wise decisions about their rights.

Any of the participants in a case—prosecutor, defense counsel, judge, or probation officer—can propose restorative justice. We believe attorneys

---

[46] Van Ness *et al.*, Restoring Justice, *supra* Chapter 7 note 44, at 61–63.

[47] Lawrence Sherman & Heather Strong, Restorative Justice: The Evidence (London: The Smith Institute, 2007) (meta-analysis of 36 studies).

should carefully consider restorative justice processes when they are available in a community. Both restoration of victims and protection of the public—two of the goals of restorative justice—should be among a prosecutor's top priorities.

Defense lawyers should present the possibility of pursuing restorative justice to clients where it is available. Restorative justice may be the means of restoring a client's relationship with a victim and restoring the client to the community. Attorneys should inform their clients whether their state treats apologies or statements in restorative justice sessions as confidential and explore whether participation in restorative justice will damage the client's prospects within the traditional system.[48] Clients can then make informed choices whether to pursue restorative justice.

Restorative justice holds out the promise of bringing peace of mind and comfort to victims and forgiveness and reconciliation to defendants. It is our hope that prosecutors and defense attorneys will serve as bridges to restorative justice.[49]

---

[48] *See* "Restorative Justice Laws," *University of Denver, Graduate School of Social Work*, accessed August 26, 2022 https://socialwork.du.edu/content/restorative-justice-laws; *see, e.g.*, Colorado Revised Statute § 18–1.3–104(b.5)(I) (2020).

[49] Robert F. Cochran Jr., *The Criminal Defense Attorney: Roadblock or Bridge to Restorative Justice*, 14 J. OF LAW AND RELIGION 211 (1999–2000).

CHAPTER 8

MERCY/CARE

■ ■ ■

On one occasion an expert in the law stood up to test Jesus. "Teacher," he asked, "what must I do to inherit eternal life?"

"What is written in the Law?" he replied. "How do you read it?"

He answered: " 'Love the Lord your God with all your heart and with all your soul and with all your strength and with all your mind,' and, 'Love your neighbor as yourself.' "

"You have answered correctly," Jesus replied. "Do this and you will live."

But he wanted to justify himself, so he asked Jesus, "And who is my neighbor?"

In reply Jesus said: "A man was going down from Jerusalem to Jericho, when he fell into the hands of robbers. They stripped him of his clothes, beat him and went away, leaving him half dead. A priest happened to be going down the same road, and when he saw the man, he passed by on the other side. So too, a Levite, when he came to the place and saw him, passed by on the other side. But a Samaritan, as he traveled, came where the man was; and when he saw him, he took pity on him. He went to him and bandaged his wounds, pouring on oil and wine. Then he put the man on his own donkey, took him to an inn and took care of him. The next day he took out two silver coins and gave them to the innkeeper. 'Look after him,' he said, 'and when I return, I will reimburse you for any extra expense you may have.'

"Which of these three do you think was a neighbor to the man who fell into the hands of robbers?"

The expert in the law replied, "The one who had mercy on him."

Jesus told him, "Go and do likewise."[1]

* * *

---

[1] Luke 10:25–37; *see also* Leviticus 19:18 and Deuteronomy 6:5.

As noted in the last chapter, Lawrence Kohlberg argues that the liberal democratic concept of justice, protection of the rights of others, encompasses all of morality. But if justice is seen as merely giving others their due, the story of the good Samaritan seems to present another concept of morality. Or, it may be that there is more to justice than Kohlberg suggests. Although the victim in the story of the good Samaritan may have had a right not to be robbed and a right to redress from the robbers, he had no "right" to the care of the Samaritan. Maybe the Samaritan acted based on some aspect of morality other than justice as we students of the law usually understand it.

Kohlberg overlooks the Jewish and Christian ethic of mercy,[2] an ethic that has much in common with the feminist ethic of care.[3] Mercy and care present a morality whose

> . . . defining aims are care, concern, and contribution to the positive development and flourishing of others. Isolation, oppression, pain, and suffering are seen as basic evils, and thus the perspective is especially responsive to needs for the basic material conditions of life, as well as for love, compassion, and fellowship. It is particularly wary of the illusion that a person's good lies in simple individual self-actualization. Moral responsiveness typically arises from recognizing need rather than right (or obligation). Need recognition, in the relevant senses, requires that others be seen as more than abstract locations of rights not to be interfered with.[4]

Whereas "[Kohlberg's ethic of justice] relies on rights, duties, individual autonomy, and generally applicable rules, [an ethic of care relies] on care, responsiveness, avoidance of harm, and interdependent relationships."[5]

An ethic of mercy is concerned with the full context of the other person as sister, brother, neighbor, or fellow human, not merely with his or her rights. Moral requirements consequent on an ethic of mercy emerge from the needs of others irrespective of what is fair, irrespective of what they

---

[2] *See* William K. Frankena, Ethics 46 (2d ed. 1973) (identifying "beneficence" as an additional part of morality).

[3] *See* Carol Gilligan, In a Different Voice: Psychological Theory and Women's Development (1982). Gilligan suggests that an ethic of care is more characteristic of women than of men. *Id.* at 79. In Carol Gilligan's analysis of the way that women deal with ethical problems—and are more inclined toward an ethic of care—she noticed that women typically did not do "well" on Kohlberg's morality tests. They were frustrated by short hypotheticals that gave them limited information and limited options. They wanted to know more about the people involved. They wanted to explore options that were not obvious and that the limitations of the test did not allow them to explore. *See id.* at 25–31; *see also* Carrie Menkel-Meadow, *Portia in a Different Voice: Speculations on a Woman's Lawyering Process*, 1 BERKELEY WOMEN'S L.J. 39, 45–47 (1985).

[4] Owen Flanagan, Varieties of Moral Personality, 203 (1991) (describing an ethic of care). *See also* Jack & Jack, Moral Vision and Professional Decisions, *supra* Chapter 1 note 32, at 1; Theresa Glennon, *Lawyers and Caring: Building an Ethic of Care into Professional Responsibility*, 43 HASTINGS L.J. 1175, 1178–79 (1992).

[5] Jack & Jack, *supra* Chapter 1 note 32.

may deserve. As a matter of social ethics, mercy seeks to avoid systemic harm to individuals—from any source—and to avoid political or legal programs that break down community. An ethic of mercy calls clients (and lawyers) to help others and may call on clients (and lawyers) to yield their rights; it may call on them to be "more than fair."

An ethic of mercy is concerned with outcomes, with the impact that decisions will have on relationships. It is concerned with the context of an individual's life in the community. Lawyers and clients who are alert to caring are likely to want to know more about the people involved, even the people on the other side. They will seek resolutions that will meet everyone's needs.

1. AN ETHIC FOR SPECIAL RELATIONSHIPS, AN ETHIC FOR ENEMIES

Part of an ethic of care that modern feminist writers have focused on, which reaches back to Cicero and, beyond him, to Hebrew scripture, teaches that we have a special responsibility to provide for the needs of those with whom we have a special relationship—including members of our families and members of our communities. For example, though the Mosaic Law, as understood by many of the Rabbis of first century Palestine, required the Israelites to provide some assistance to the "alien," it required them to provide greater levels of assistance to their fellow Jews. Steven Wexler's story of the women who accosted the doctor out of concern for one of their malnourished children (Chapter Two) appears to be the story of a mother who exercised an ethic of care toward her child, at the expense of the just claims of the doctor and the hospital's other patients. An ethic of mercy and an ethic of care point to a special concern for those with whom we have organic or communal relationships, but care for these special others can lead us also to care for those beyond our communities. Our religious traditions teach us to care, even for our enemies. This is an aspect of the story of the Good Samaritan, one that is easy for us to miss. It was apparently a matter of argument among the Rabbis in Jesus's time. The lawyer who asked, "Who is my neighbor?" was probably concerned about the extent of his duty of care. (A modern lawyer might ask, "Is the opposing party my neighbor?") If the lawyer wanted Jesus to place limits on his duty, the lawyer must have been disappointed. For the man who helped the injured traveler was not merely a stranger; he was a Samaritan, one of a racial group whom many in Jesus's Galilee hated.

What Jesus left wonderfully implicit in the story of the Good Samaritan, he made explicit in his Sermon on the Mount. "Love your enemies, do good to those who hate you."[6] Jesus was there paraphrasing a verse from the Book of Proverbs—"If thine enemy be hungry, give him

[6] Luke 6:27.

bread to eat; and if he be thirsty, give him water to drink. For thou shalt heap coals of fire upon his head, and the Lord shall reward thee."[7] The Rabbis understood the coals of fire to be metaphorical—shame at being hostile, maybe. Rabbi Hanina bar Hama explicated the verse this way: "[E]ven if the enemy came to your house to slay you, and he is hungry or thirsty, give him food and drink; for thereby God will reconcile him to you."[8]

2. RELATIONSHIPS AND RECONCILIATION

The goal of reconciliation, expressed by Rabbi Hanina bar Hama, highlights another aspect of the ethics of mercy and care, the importance of relationships. As Martin Buber said, we come to *be* in relationships. We are not the autonomous, lonely individuals celebrated by liberal democracy. We are connected to and dependent on one another. A feminist image is that of the web.[9] A Christian image is that of the body: Those in the church are parts of one body.[10] As Paul Zwier and Ann Hamric have argued, an ethic of care is particularly appropriate when the lawyer acts for multiple parties with potentially conflicting interests (e.g., drafting corporate documents or partnership agreements), when the lawyer acts as trustee for trusts with multiple beneficiaries, and when families are at the center of the controversy (including legal problems concerning the guardianship and care of children and the elderly, as well as bioethical issues).[11]

In the context of legal conflict, Rabbi Hanina bar Hama's message is that the client should care for the opposing party in the hope of reconciliation. The contrast between the family trust story (Chapter One) and the family business story (Chapter Four) illustrates the difference in the importance of relationships under a narrow perception of justice and under a perception of mercy. Let us assume that in each story there was some legitimacy to the claim of the client. In both cases, the clients went to lawyers who prepared to file suit against the opposing family member.

The family trust story illustrates what filing suit often does to relationships. Ned's lawyers filed suit. Ned was reduced to writing his brother Sam a letter saying that the accusations in the suit were "very far from representing my feelings toward you." Not surprisingly, "Sam was offended deeply by being accused of breach of trust" and refused to settle. Ned's lawyers played what has become a common role for lawyers in the United States. Lawyers stand between the client and the opponent; they free clients from the responsibilities of relationships and in the process

---

7 Proverbs 25:21–22.

8 *Quoted in* Samuel S. Cohon, Judaism: A Way of Life 214 n. (1948).

9 *See* Gilligan, *supra* Chapter 8 note 3, at 62; *see also* Menkel-Meadow, *supra* Chapter 8 note 3, at 59.

10 *See* I Corinthians 12.

11 *See* Paul Zwier & Ann B. Hamric, *The Ethics of Care and ReImagining the Lawyer/Client Relationship*, 22 J. CONTEMP. L. 383, 431–32 (1996).

destroy the relationships. After several days of grueling cross-examination, Sam died.

Sam's and Ned's family trust dispute stands in sharp contrast to the story of the family business dispute: Johnson's son-in-law, Warren, had purchased Johnson's interest in their jointly owned business. The business was the source of their dispute. As is often the case, the dispute between the parties affected not only their relationship but a web of relationships, including Johnson's daughter (Warren's wife) and Johnson's grandchildren (Warren's children). Johnson's second lawyer, Robert Whitfield, talked to Johnson about the likely consequences of litigation. Whitfield "secured Johnson's promise to call off the lawsuit, thus substituting a process of compromise for one of conflict. In this new process, assertion of rights would be secondary to accommodation." They reached settlement, and Whitfield hoped that the settlement would clear the way for Johnson, Warren, and their family to be reconciled. In this case, the lawyer served as an agent of reconciliation, rather than exacerbating the rift between the parties.

The story of the Catholic Church and sexual abuse (Chapter One) presents a similar situation in which the lawyer's focus was adversarial advocacy and litigation rather than reconciliation, even though the victims of the priests' sexual abuse had a relationship with the Catholic Church that needed mending.

Reconciliation as a lawyer and client goal will affect the way that they attempt to settle a dispute. We do not know the manner in which Whitfield negotiated the settlement of the family business dispute, but we suspect that he did not use "hard ball" tactics. Negotiation can be adversarial or conciliatory. Negotiation that is conciliatory in both style and tactics is most likely to lead to reconciliation as well as settlement.[12] Had the lawyers for the Catholic Church considered reconciliation as a goal rather than focusing on "victory," that might have helped mend relationships and possibly saved significant financial resources for a number of Dioceses.

Another method of dispute resolution that may lead to reconciliation is mediation, in which the parties sit down with a mediator who helps them reach agreement. Mediation can take place in the civil community or in the religious congregation.[13] In mediation, the parties to the dispute frequently deal with one another face to face. The mediator seeks to enable each of them to understand the other. This can stimulate empathy, which can lead to resolution of the dispute and even reconciliation. The parties explore options that meet the needs of both of the parties, but that courts would

[12] Cochran, *Legal Representatives and Client Control, supra* Chapter 1 note 16, at 859–601.

[13] For a discussion of dispute resolution within religious communities, *see* Andrew W. McThenia & Thomas L. Shaffer, *For Reconciliation*, 94 YALE L.J. 1660, 1665–68 (1985). For the suggestion that alternative means of dispute resolution are consistent with a feminist care ethic, *see* Menkel-Meadow, *supra* Chapter 8 note 3, at 52–53.

have no power to order. Such a process is more likely to lead to reconciliation of the parties than litigation, which is likely to drive the parties apart.[14]

There are many other methods of dispute resolution that a lawyer might discuss with a client, but we will highlight one more—Collaborative Practice.[15] Collaborative Practice has proven to be especially helpful in family cases. In Collaborative Practice, the clients and their attorneys, and a counselor in some cases, contract to resolve the issues presented in the case in a structured process without litigation. Both sets of clients and lawyers agree to:

- Negotiate a mutually acceptable settlement without having courts decide issues;
- Maintain open communication and information sharing; and
- Create shared solutions, acknowledging the highest priorities of all affected persons.

In addition, they agree that the lawyers will withdraw from the case if the matter proceeds to litigation. The threat that both parties will lose their attorneys and that litigation will resume appears to create new impetus for peaceful resolution.

3. THE DOMINANCE OF AN ETHIC OF RIGHTS IN THE LAW OFFICE

It may be difficult for lawyers to practice the sort of peacemaking that mercy contemplates. It is not that lawyers don't know how to show mercy, but that somehow they do not show mercy *as lawyers*. They know that moral requirements emerge from the needs of others, irrespective even of what is fair. They know that an ethic of mercy seeks to avoid breaking down community, irrespective of client rights. They know that peacemaking may call on clients to help the suffering opponent, and may even call on them to yield their rights. They know that what they do for their clients may have broad economic and political effects. But what they know is somehow left at the law-office door.

Though an ethic of mercy is a rich and important ethic for the law office, it may be drowned out by an ethic of rights. As we have suggested in several places in this book, the dominant model of law office discourse, a communication between the professional advocate and the autonomous client, expresses an ethic of rights. The professional advocate determines what is in the financial interest of the client and asserts this as a *right* of

---

[14] *See* Cochran, *supra* Chapter 8 note 12, at 865 & 869.

[15] Cochran, *Collaborative Practice Ethics*, *supra* Chapter 1 note 13, at 537–567.

the client—the client is a bundle of rights.[16] The focus is on doing what will make and keep the client free from interference from other people. Rights talk has become the dominant form of law office discourse for several reasons.

First, Americans find it difficult to discuss issues from a perspective that emphasizes mercy. Sociologist Robert Bellah and his colleagues, in a study of the moral values of Americans, found that most Americans act from a combination of individualistic and community orientations,[17] but that the language of individualism comes most easily to them. Americans are quick to speak of morality in terms of one's rights, but our actions show a greater concern for community and for others than our language of individualism would indicate. For Americans, care for others is one of the "habits of the heart" (Toqueville's phrase, adopted as the title of Bellah's book). Of course, if lawyers and clients leave the caring habits of their hearts at home they are likely to resolve issues in the law office primarily based on an ethic of rights.

Second, it may be that the historic control by men of the legal profession has led to a dominance of an ethic of rights in the law office. Though it is common for both men and women to respond at times with an ethic of rights and at times with an ethic of care, Carol Gilligan and others have found that care is a more persistent vision of morality in women than in men.[18]

With the dramatic increase in the number of women in law school in recent decades, one might expect to see a tendency toward care reasoning in the law office as women become more influential in law firms and law associations. Sadly, however, it appears that lawyers who normally have a care orientation in their personal morality, whether male or female, tend to evaluate legal problems from a rights perspective. In their interviews with both male and female lawyers, Rand Jack and Dana Crowley Jack found that, "The more the interview fixed attorneys in their legal role, the more they talked like lawyers and the less care thinking was visible."[19]

A final explanation for the dominance of an ethic of rights in the law office can be found in law school education. As noted previously, law school training focuses on rights and "thinking like a lawyer" at the expense of care and mercy.[20] Law schools primarily train students to assert rights,

---

[16] For thoughtful critiques of the tendency of Americans to view everything in terms of rights, *see* Mary Ann Glendon, Rights Talk (1991) and Robert Rodes, Law and Liberation 38–51 (1986).

[17] *See* Bellah *et al.*, Habits of the Heart, *supra* Chapter 4 note 8. We take "individualism," as Bellah and his colleagues use the term, to be equivalent to what we are calling an ethic of rights.

[18] Gilligan, *supra* Chapter 8 note 3, at 79. *See also* Jack & Jack, *supra* Chapter 1 note 32, at 56.

[19] Jack & Jack, *supra* Chapter 1 note 32, at 56.

[20] *See* Cramton, *supra* Chapter 1 note 6; Glennon, *supra* Chapter 8 note 4, at 1176–77; *see also* Mertz, *supra* Chapter 4 note 21.

and to view legal problems from the perspective of adversaries. Legal education generally assumes that the interests of communities must be subordinated to individual rights.

We, however, agree with Paul Zwier and Ann Hamric:

> [W]here the situation involves individuals in strong relationships with each other, it makes sense that early involvement of others is crucial both to gathering accurate information and to understanding what care demands of the people involved. It strikes us that such a system encourages us to be our sisters' and brothers' keepers. It requires us to at least be facilitators of relationships and, thus, healing forces in the community. It would require the lawyer to break out of the bounds of rights-analysis and seek to find particularized human solutions that better fit the people involved.[21]

4. RECONCILING THE DEMANDS OF JUSTICE AND MERCY

Much of the conflict that is commonly perceived between an ethic of justice and an ethic of mercy springs, we believe, from an Enlightenment perception of justice, a perception of justice as the right to be autonomous, the right to be free to "do my own thing." A duty to be merciful would conflict with such a right. But the biblical perception of justice includes both rights and responsibilities, both the individual and the community, both the community at hand and all of God's children. Jewish and Christian scripture praise both justice and mercy, suggesting that they are two sides of the coin of biblical morality: "He has told you, O mortal, what is good; and what does the LORD require of you but to do justice, and to love kindness, and to walk humbly with your God?"[22] It may be that the Jewish and Christian conception of justice is different, broader than that of the Enlightenment, or it may be merely that biblical morality calls on people to be more than just—it calls on them to show mercy as well.

Generally, the demands of mercy are the same as, or, at least consistent with, those of biblical justice. The Mosaic Law is full of laws that require mercy *as* justice—farmers are to leave part of the crop on the field for the poor; workers are to be paid before sunset; money is to be loaned without interest; every fifty years land is to be returned to the families that originally owned it.[23] To fail to abide by these laws of the Torah was a denial of justice, just as it would have been a failure to exercise mercy. Repeatedly, the Hebrew prophets demand that the nation give justice to

---

[21] Zwier & Hamric, *supra* Chapter 8 note 11, at 433.

[22] Micah 6:8.

[23] *See supra* text accompanying Chapter Seven note 8.

the helpless: the orphan, the widow, and the alien. The Hebrew word for justice can be translated as "righteousness"—all of morality.

In some cases, however, the demands of justice may seem to conflict with the demands of mercy. This is likely to arise in cases in which justice is on the side of the client, but the opposing party or some third party is in substantial need or may suffer disproportionate damage as the result of an action the client or lawyer might take.

Some of the great Jewish teachers, including Jesus and Rabbi Hillel, said that the moral law, which would include the demands of justice and mercy, could be summed up in the commandment to love your neighbor as yourself. In the context of legal representation, it may be that clients are called on to treat the opposing party as they would treat themselves. Most of the time, people want to be treated fairly, to get what justice would afford them; therefore, as a general rule, it may be that the demands of justice can resolve the issues lawyer and client face. But, if we are in real need we want to have our need met whether we "deserve" to have it met or not. So it may be that when the other person is in substantial need, that need should trump what seem to be the demands of justice.

That, of course, does not tell us what to do in all situations in which an ethic of justice seems to conflict with an ethic of care. Steven Wexler's story about the malnourished child (Chapter Two) raises this problem. In that case the client was faced with conflict between her child's need for medical care and the interests of the doctor and the other patients of the hospital. This was a case in which the mother's responsibilities of care to the child were great. She had a special relationship with the child and the child was in great need. An ethic of care may have called her to pursue the interests of her child, but an ethic of justice may have said the doctor had a right to pursue his work, the other patients who had been waiting a long time had a right to see him, and the patients who would come first to the clinic on Monday morning had a right to see the doctor first.

We do not offer an answer to the issue that the lawyer and client would have faced had they wrestled with the client's conflicting responsibilities. If the client loved her child, the doctor, and the other patients as she loved herself, it is not clear what she would have done. Our argument is that they should have wrestled with it—that at the very least the lawyer should have, by expressing his own misgivings, invited his client to think about the other patients.

Discussions of mercy do not come easily in the law office. Our argument is that lawyers should raise the issue, and that raising it is not imposing their morality on clients. Lawyers should issue an invitation to talk about mercy. At a minimum, they should not discourage clients' care-based moral impulses. We suggested in Chapter Five that lawyers raise issues of justice by asking whether each option considered would be fair to other persons who might be affected. An ethic of mercy can be brought into the conversation by identifying the harm each option might cause to others and asking whether there is a way that harm can be avoided. The lawyer can at least ask clients *whether* they would like to try and find a solution that would not cause harm to others.

When the ethics of justice and mercy seem to clash, the lawyer and client may have some difficult issues to resolve, but no one has suggested that the moral life is an easy life. We human beings seem to have been put together—and put with one another—so that we can talk about such things and help one another with them.

5. NONRESISTANCE

The religious traditions of Jews and Christians counsel not in terms of rights, but in terms that seem to go beyond the demands of the modern conception of justice. The religious traditions speak of living with neighbors in a peace that is so radical that it will not be controlled by the demands of the law, even when those demands operate in the believer's favor. This ethic says that believers should forego the legal power they have in order to demonstrate the grace and generosity with which God created the universe.

Whereas mercy encourages the client to look out for those who might be injured by actions taken during legal representation, there is moral teaching in our inheritance that goes even beyond mercy—a principle and practice of nonresistance that calls for subordination, even to a domineering adversary. In the Sermon on the Mount, Jesus says, "[D]o not resist him who is evil. . . . If someone sues you for your coat, give him your cloak; if someone demands that you walk one mile, go two."[24] Jesus uses two illustrations to teach that his followers should give to others even more than they demand. The reference to the lawsuit presents an issue that might be faced by a lawyer and a client: In the context of litigation, the implication is that one should go beyond the demands of others. The second, the "walk a mile" illustration, is more obscure, perhaps, but, when explained, it is even more demanding: Roman law allowed a Roman soldier to stop others and require that they carry the soldier's pack for a mile. This was a law that the Jews resented and saw as unjust, particularly so as the Romans were an occupying army in their Promised Land. Jesus taught that they should carry the Roman military baggage an additional mile. This second illustration suggests that we should go beyond even the unjust demands of our adversaries.

We might dismiss the full implications of these statements as hyperbole. Jesus did use hyperbole—at another time he said, "If anyone comes to me and does not hate his own father and mother and wife and

[24] Matthew 5:39–41.

children . . . he cannot be my disciple." But even if we view the statements about giving up the cloak and walking an extra mile as hyperbole, they illustrate a difficult moral teaching. Just as the teaching about hating one's family emphasizes the degree of the love we are to have for God, the other statements teach us something about how we are to deal with adversaries. We should be willing to give up, not demand, our rights. American Christians generally have neglected this teaching on nonresistance—with the notable exceptions of those in the Anabaptist wing of the Protestant Reformation (the Amish, Mennonites, and others) and those in the civil rights movement of the 1960s.

In our rights-oriented society it may seem odd even to ask whether people should assert their rights. We tend to view the assertion of rights as a duty. In one case, for example, the owner of a restaurant denied service to the plaintiff because of a disputed bill of one dollar. The New York Court of Appeals held that the plaintiff was entitled to recover. Justice Cardozo said,

> It is no concern of ours that the controversy at the root of this lawsuit may seem to be trivial. . . . To enforce one's rights when they are violated is never a legal wrong, *and may often be a moral duty*. It happens in many instances that the violation passes with no effort to redress it—sometimes from praiseworthy forbearance, sometimes from weakness, sometimes from mere inertia. But the law which creates a right, can certainly not concede that an insistence upon its enforcement is evidence of a wrong.[25]

There are moral arguments for Cardozo's point of view: Many of the legally enforced rights that we enjoy today are present because others insisted on those rights in the past. They may be lost to our descendants if we fail to assert them for ourselves. We Americans, however, are quick to see the assertion of a right as a "legal duty" and slow to see nonresistance as "praiseworthy forbearance."

The morality of nonresistance sounds particularly impractical in abstract discussions of business practice; even so, some business people practice such an ethic and discuss with lawyers what the ethic requires of them. They surrender not only their rights as defined by laws such as the statute of frauds, but also surrender objection to what the person making a demand on them seems to want. The experience of mediators, particularly those who work in religion-based programs of reconciliation, frequently includes such stories.

We recall such a story from the experience of Anabaptist Americans. The neighbor of a prosperous Amish farmer, in Lancaster County, Pennsylvania, appeared at the farmer's door one day to say that the

[25] *Morningstar v. Lafayette Hotel Co.*, 211 N.Y. 465, 105 N.E. 656 (1914) (emphasis added).

property line between this farmer's farm and the neighbor's farm had been drawn wrong, and that the correction would operate in the Amish farmer's favor and against the neighbor. The farmer asked his neighbor to show him where the line should be and the two of them walked to the fence between their farms. The Amish farmer looked his neighbor in the eye and said the line would be wherever the neighbor said it should be. (We heard that story from the lawyer son of the Amish farmer. The son said the story worried him because it showed undue power in his father's ethic. To this lawyer son it seemed that putting the neighbor to his own practice of justice—or, perhaps, of nonresistance—put too heavy a moral demand on the neighbor.)

There is a legitimate debate as to whether Jews and Christians should ever go to court. John Calvin, a leader of the Protestant Reformation, who was trained as a lawyer, celebrated judges as a gift from God, whose purpose is to protect us from injustice and enable us to live peaceful lives.[26] Our point is that the argument for nonresistance is seldom heard in modern America, that it is worth taking into account in the law office, and that lawyers who hear faint murmurs of it from their clients should listen to and consider and even encourage what they hear. This is a part of our moral inheritance that should not be shouted down by lawyers.

6. ATTITUDES TOWARD OPPONENTS

John Calvin defended the use of the courts, but he also had some advice about the way a client should approach litigation. His description of litigants could have been written today:

> There are very many who so boil with a rage for litigation that they are never at peace with themselves unless they are quarreling with others. And they carry on their lawsuits with bitter and deadly hatred, and an insane passion to revenge and hurt, and they pursue them with implacable obstinacy even to the ruin of their adversaries. Meanwhile, to avoid being thought of as doing something wrong, they defend such perversity on the pretense of legal procedure. [Rights!] But if one is permitted to go to law with a brother, one is not therewith allowed to hate him, or be seized with a mad desire to harm him, or hound him relentlessly. . . .
>
> [A] lawsuit, however just, can never be rightly prosecuted by any man, unless he treat his adversary with the same love and good will as if the business under controversy were already amicably settled and composed. Perhaps someone will interpose here that such moderation is so uniformly absent from any lawsuit

---

[26] *See* John Calvin, The Institutes (1536) (Walter G. Hardos Trans., 1955), *reprinted in* John Calvin: Selections From His Writings 492 (John Dillenberger ed., 1971).

> that it would be a miracle if any such were found. Indeed, I admit that, as the customs of these times go, an example of an upright litigant is rare; but the thing itself, when not corrupted by the addition of anything evil, does not cease to be good and pure. But when we hear that the help of the [judge] is a holy gift of God, we must more diligently guard against its becoming polluted by our fault.[27]

Many lawyers believe that a client's attitude toward litigation is no concern of the lawyer. This opinion, we believe, rests on an impoverished perception of the interests of the client. Hate corrodes. A client who acts in hatred acts not only to the detriment of the opposing party, but to the detriment of the client as well. Litigators know clients who are destroyed by lawsuits; whether they win or lose, they are consumed by an obsession with their rights.

We think that John Calvin's warning—the love-one-another condition he put on otherwise legitimate litigation—is something lawyers should discuss with their clients. If nothing else, lawyers can point out to clients—as many do—what the hatred a lawsuit might encourage can do to the client and the client's relationships. Recall the story of the family business dispute. The lawyer, Robert Whitfield, noted that his client, who was prepared to sue his son-in-law and an old friend, "seemed seriously agitated, and [Whitfield concluded] that the litigation would exaggerate his agitation and continue it far into the future." Whitfield told his client that "he could either spend the rest of his life stewing about it or he could move on."

Lawyers should—we think—talk to clients about the risk that if they allow their competitive attitude toward the opposing party to have full reign, it will develop into destructive, corrosive hatred. Too often lawyers have an opposite impact. Too often lawyers fan the lames of hostility. Maybe lawyers do that in order to convince their clients that they will be aggressive advocates. Maybe they do it because they know that litigation is debilitating, that it takes stamina to pursue a lawsuit, and that ill will builds stamina.

Calvin's teaching for such possibilities is subtle and, in some ways, more difficult than the teaching of the Anabaptist tradition and the tradition in Judaism that believers should refrain altogether from civil litigation. In any event, it seems to us that Calvin's warning requires conversation between lawyer and client and, perhaps, creative suggestions (of a moral sort) from lawyers. A saving attitude here, for example, may be Calvin's suggestion that the parties take the case to the judge and, whether they win or lose, trust the judge to give a just decision.[28] Or—we think even

---

[27] *Id.* at 492–93.

[28] *See id.*

better—that they take the case to a third party who can appeal to the parties' common interests and help them to reconcile.

A client's attitude toward the other party is important, not only because hatred can consume the client, but because love can transform the other party. Martin Luther King, Jr. is one who loved those who treated him unjustly. As Benjamin Mays said at Dr. King's funeral:

> If any man knew the meaning of suffering, King knew. House bombed; living day by day for thirteen years under constant threats of death; maliciously accused of being a Communist; falsely accused of being insincere . . .; stabbed by a member of his own race; slugged in a hotel lobby; jailed over twenty times; occasionally deeply hurt because friends betrayed him—and yet this man had no bitterness in his heart, no rancour in his soul, no revenge in his mind; and he went up and down the length and breadth of this world preaching non-violence and the redemptive power of love."[29]

In a sermon written in a Georgia jail, Dr. King said "hate multiplies hate" and is "just as injurious to the person who hates" as to the one who is hated. "[L]ove is the only force that is capable of transforming an enemy into a friend."[30] These are challenging words, but words that we believe have a place in the law office.

---

[29] Coretta Scott King, My Life With Martin Luther King, Jr. 365–69 (1970), *quoted in* John R.W. Stott, The Message of the Sermon on the Mount 114 (1978).

[30] Martin Luther King, Jr., Strength to Love 47–55 (1969), *quoted in* Stott, *supra* Chapter 8 note 29.

CHAPTER 9

TRUTHFULNESS

■ ■ ■

1. THE SOCIAL SECURITY CLAIM

We begin our consideration of truthfulness in the law office with a story based on a case in which one of us served as an attorney:

* * *

Irma Jenkins is a client with a claim under the federal Supplemental Security Income (S.S.I.) program administered by the Social Security Administration (S.S.A.). She has retained me to lead her through the last phase of the administrative appeal system maintained by S.S.A., in an effort to receive S.S.I. benefits based on her physical impairment—on, as the law says, total and permanent disability. When we complete this phase, if the result is not favorable to my client, we will have exhausted administrative remedies; we may then take the case to federal court.

Irma is 55 years old and unmarried. She was married once early in her life, but the marriage ended in divorce in less than two years. She has a daughter from that marriage. Six months ago, Irma had open-heart surgery, to repair damage to her heart that, her doctors said, would have caused her death. She has recovered from the surgery, more or less, but is left with shortness of breath that keeps her from working on her feet for long periods of time, with chronic nervousness, and with a tendency to get backaches from working while seated.

None of the medical evidence in the record I have assembled for Irma is as convincing as I would like: Her cardiac surgeon says Irma should avoid strenuous activity. Irma has seen an orthopedic surgeon about her back, but the best we can get from him is the opinion that the back pain is due to muscle spasms; he cannot say whether the condition is permanent.

We may end up depending mainly on an argument based on Irma's age and the fact that she has never really been in the employment market: She was a homemaker until her daughter grew up, then worked for short periods of time as a waitress. That, and such medical evidence as we have, give us, in my opinion, a fighting chance to win the case. The essence of the case is going to be that Irma cannot work. Irma can explain that to an administrative law judge, and she will be a good witness—positively pathetic, in fact.

The difficulty of the case, from Irma's—or any Social Security client's—point of view, has been aggravated by the system: People who go to Social Security offices to file S.S.I. claims usually find the people there friendly and helpful at filling out the forms and submitting the evidence for a first-level determination. But they usually find that their applications are denied at the first level; applicants then tend to say, "Social Security says I am not disabled." An appeal for bureaucratic reconsideration, a second look by the disability determination agency, usually repeats the denial of the application. At the third level, the administrative hearing, judges often overrule the administrators. At some points in Social Security's recent history, administrative law judges have reversed more than half of the determinations made at the lower two levels.

But many applicants give up along the way. Some of those who do not give up come to lawyers, which is what Irma did. I filed a request for hearing for her; her case is pending before an administrative law judge. We expect to go to the hearing within the next month. But Irma is not optimistic, in view of the fact that she has been turned down twice. My cheerleader's advice on the chances before the judge has not kept her from being discouraged.

Meanwhile, she tries to get by. There is no regular or dependable source of assistance for her from state agencies: Her daughter is grown and away from home; Irma is no longer eligible for welfare assistance under the Aid to Families with Dependent Children (A.F.D.C.) program. Our state last year abolished its program of assistance for single people. Irma gets $112 a month in food stamps from the local welfare office. She would have no food for the last week of some months but for the fact that her adult daughter, who receives A.F.D.C., and people from her church bring her food during these times.

Irma covers the rent on her humble, neat, upstairs apartment by what I am afraid may be surreptitious employment: Every night, she cleans out the tavern that is on the street level under her apartment, after the tavern closes at about 1 a.m., and, for this, the tavern owner (who is also her landlord) waives the rent called for in her lease—$200 a month. This midnight-shift work is not easy for Irma: She finds she can sweep or mop for about 20 minutes and then has to lie down on a cot in the back of the tavern for half an hour before she can get back to work. It often takes her until 5 a.m. to finish cleaning the place. But she always gets it done.

Irma at first did not tell me about this tavern-cleaning arrangement. I learned what I know mostly from talking to the tavern owner one day when I went by Irma's apartment to get her to sign a Social Security form, and from a telephone conversation with Irma's daughter.

When Irma initially applied for S.S.I., a friendly person in the Social Security Office helped her fill out a detailed "application for supplemental security income" form. This occurred long before Irma consulted me. Although, arguably, there are several places on that form where her arrangement for cleaning the tavern might have been disclosed, the filled-in form does not disclose what she does in return for her rent waiver. Apparently, the official at the Social Security office did not ask Irma questions that would have caused Irma to talk about that arrangement, and the filled-in form says that she is unemployed. Irma is not the sort of person who would tell a lie.

I have worked in the following statement in one of the letters I put into the record: "The applicant gets consideration on the rent for her apartment by occasional help with cleaning the building in which she lives." That is the truth, certainly; I wrote the letter in good conscience. But I have lately begun to worry over the fact that this statement is far from the whole truth. The whole truth, as I see it, is that Irma earns the equivalent of $200 a month, every month, by working up to five hours in the middle of the night, six days a week. If the judge were to see that as establishing that Irma can work, the judge's order could keep Irma from receiving S.S.I.

I have twice paused, with some discomfort, over the statement that appears above Irma's signature on the application form: "I/We understand that anyone who knowingly lies or misrepresents the truth or arranges for someone to knowingly lie or misrepresent the truth is committing a crime which can be punished under Federal law, State law, or both. Everything on this application is the truth as best I/we know it." On the other hand, it is possible to go through the form, item by item, and to contend that there is nothing clearly false in it and no failure to provide the information the form asks for. It is certainly the case that Irma answered truthfully all of the questions the official in the Social Security office asked.

It is even possible to argue that the form does not call for disclosure of Irma's arrangement with the tavern owner. And, in any case, it might be that Irma could fully disclose her arrangement with the tavern owner and still get S.S.I. For example, we could contend before the judge that it is harmful and painful for Irma to clean the tavern; she needs S.S.I. so that she can stop staying up at night to clean the tavern. Or, for another example, it could be that her "earnings" from cleaning the tavern would not constitute the amount and type of "income" that would disqualify Irma for S.S.I. benefits. Still, I am confident that if the judge at the hearing asks Irma questions that call for her to disclose the tavern-cleaning arrangement, Irma will be confused and embarrassed. Maybe, in view of what the "whole truth" is, she (and I) *should be* confused and embarrassed.

On the other hand, Irma's is a desperate case: She is one of God's poor. She is, in essence, one of the widows the Hebrew prophets talk about in the Bible—and only God knows how long she can continue to clean the tavern. I cannot predict how the administrative law judge will regard information about Irma's cleaning the tavern, if the judge has it. I cannot count on the medical evidence alone to convince the judge that Irma is totally and permanently disabled. Her case may need the persuasive force of the picture of her as a pitiable old woman, virtually unable to do anything to support herself.

* * *

2. THE PRINCIPLE OF TRUTH

Virtually all systems of ethics say that truthfulness is fundamental to personal, professional, and social morality. Irma's "system" would say that: She would not tell a lie. She apparently does not believe that she has told a lie: If what is written in the blanks of her Social Security application lies, it does so by the accident of her not having filled out the form herself and her not having read it carefully before she signed it. She did not "knowingly" (the adverb that appears twice on the Social Security form) make a false statement. Whether the form presents the whole truth or not—and that has to be talked about—Irma did not tell a lie. The real issue is whether she now has to tell the truth to the administrative law judge.

Children, through such stories as George Washington and the cherry tree, or Pinocchio's nose, are formed in the virtue of truthfulness. The law makes lying to the government a crime—as the Social Security form says—and uses perjury prosecutions as a way to punish business persons and government officials for misbehavior it cannot reach in other ways. Immanuel Kant was so absolute in reasoning that it is immoral to lie that he would not permit a lie to save a life.[1] In Irma's ethical system of biblical morality, truth is fundamental in obedience to a God Who is described as Truth:

> When we speak of the sanctity of truth in relation to ethics, we have particularly in view "truthfulness" on our part in our dealings with God, ourselves, and [other people]. The necessity of truthfulness rests upon God's truthfulness. As we are to be holy because God is holy, so we are to be truthful because God is truthful. . . . [N]othing exemplifies the contradiction of God and of [human] integrity more than the lie. . . . The foundations of all equity are destroyed when truth has fallen. It was the lament of the prophet that "none pleadeth in truth," that "truth is fallen in the street, and equity cannot enter. Yea, truth faileth; and he that departeth from evil maketh himself a prey."[2]

The Bible develops this theme through both stories and principles. The stories include negative examples such as the lie told by the brothers of the patriarch Joseph after they sold him into slavery and the lie told by Potiphar's wife, in Egypt, when Joseph became a servant in her household and she attempted to seduce him. The principles turn on the imitation of God as a Jewish and Christian religious ideal, and on the development of truthfulness as a good habit, a virtue: Love, St. Paul says, rejoices in the truth.[3]

Both principle and story in biblical ethics relate truth telling to relationships—not only the relationship between God and each of us and our communities, but also, and more indicatively for our purposes, to the relationships between and among people. The prophet Zechariah said, "Speak ye every [person] the truth to his neighbor; execute the judgment of truth and peace in your gates: and let none of you imagine evil in your hearts . . . and love no false oath: for all these are things that I hate, saith the Lord."[4] St. Paul, in his letter to the church in Ephesus, said, "Wherefore, having put away lying, speak every [person] truth with his neighbor: for we are members of one another."[5]

Any ethical teaching that is so emphatic ends up in reasoning over what is truth and what is not—often complex reasoning that we find in both biblical ethics and modern philosophical ethics. Consider, for example, the definition that is used by the biblical scholar we quoted above, John Murray: "Ordinarily, at least, the person who is to be branded as a liar is

---

1 Sissela Bok, Lying: Moral Choice in Public and Private Life 39–46 (3d ed. 1999) (discussing Kant's essay "On a Supposed Right to Lie").

2 John Murray, Principles of Conduct: Aspects of Biblical Ethics 127 (1957), *quoting* Isaiah 59: 4, 14, 15.

3 1 Corinthians 13:6.

4 Zechariah 8:16–17.

5 Ephesians 4:25.

the person who affirms to be true what he knows or believes to be false or affirms to be false what he knows or believes to be true."[6] In framing this definition, Murray notes some distinctions.

One distinction is that between what is said and what is understood. A benign example, from the lore of lawyers, is the legal fiction. In legal fiction, as in irony, the speaker has no intention to deceive: The common-law lawyer said in his writ that his client lost his purse and the defendant found it, when the true assertion, as everyone knew, was that the defendant stole the purse.[7]

The statement Irma's lawyer carefully crafted for her S.S.I. file was meant to create the impression that she did a little sweeping in the hall and sometimes, as a consequence, got a cut in her rent; it is perhaps a less benign example of the difference between what is said and what is understood. It is perhaps like the story of Elisha the prophet and the army of the Syrian king. The Syrians were trying to find (and kill) him. Elisha let the Syrians think he was someone else, and said, "This is not the way, neither is this the city; follow me, and I will bring you to the man whom ye seek. And he led them to Samaria." Murray says, "[Elisha, standing outside the city,] may have meant, 'This is not the city in which you will find' the man whom you seek." "Let it be granted, that the Syrians understood Elisha's words in a way entirely different from Elisha's intent, does it follow that Elisha spoke untruth?"[8] Murray's answer is that Elisha was not a liar:

> Elisha was under no obligation to inform them that he was the man whom they sought. . . . We have no right to insist that the understanding of the Syrians at the time of its having been made should have dictated the sense of Elisha's statement. The meaning of Elisha's words is to be understood in the light of all the facts.[9]

Murray's answer is also based in part on a second distinction, a distinction between the hearer who is entitled to the truth and the hearer who is not. Murray argues that the Syrians were not entitled to the truth.[10] If Irma's lawyer is to be able to take advantage of Elisha's example, it may be necessary to compare his purposes with the prophet's purposes, to wonder whether "beating the system" in Irma's behalf is like leading the murderous Syrian army away from its intended victim. The principle

---

6 Murray, *supra* Chapter 9 note 2, at 133.

7 For a discussion of how lawyers are trained to be both truthful and insincere (in their role as advocates), see Lawrence M. Solan, *Lawyers as Insincere (But Truthful) Actors*, 36 J. LEGAL PROF. 487 (2012).

8 Murray, *supra* Chapter 9 note 2, at 142.

9 *Id.* at 142–43.

10 *Id.* at 147.

would be that, while it is not all right to lie, it is all right to mislead an unworthy opponent in an unfair system.

But Murray distinguishes between those who forfeit their entitlement to the truth and those who forfeit their entitlement, as human persons, not to be lied to. He suggests that there is no one who has forfeited the entitlement not to be lied to.[11] His reasoning will not let us get away with saying that a lie is all right if good will come of it. The biblical example of Rebecca, who lied in order to get an inheritance for her son Jacob, who became the patriarch of Israel, is taken by most believers to be a case where God brought good out of evil, not a case where evil was all right because good resulted.

A third distinction that might affect Irma's decision is between what is said and what is not said. Answers on the S.S.A. form to questions about employers (answer: none), income (answer: none), gifts (answer: none), wages (answer: none), and self-employment (answer: none) might, in some reasoning, be false, but Irma did not utter any lies. The answers were accidental, the product of, at worst, bureaucratic sloppiness by the person who helped Irma in the Social Security office. It is, as a bit of human behavior, innocent. The distinction between what is said and what is not said would (might) say that Irma's or her lawyer's not correcting the error is not itself a lie, but is a matter of not saying anything at all. That was—for those familiar with the story and the play—the position taken by Sir Thomas More on King Henry's Oath of Supremacy. (Another example is Atticus Finch in the scene on the porch in the movie version of "To Kill a Mockingbird," which we discuss below.)

Thinkers who appeal to the distinction between what is said and what is not said also have to appeal to other ethical reasoning—to a principle that has to do with ethics other than the ethics of truth telling (as, in Irma's case, she and her lawyer are trying to find a way to feed the poor). Based on this further ethical reasoning, a person might deceive by not telling the whole story.

3. THE VIRTUE OF TRUTHFULNESS

Those, such as John Murray, who treat truth as a principle identify rules and distinctions among rules. Such an approach can be compared with that which views truthfulness as a virtue or a good habit. We explore this virtue with a look at the behavior of the gentleman-lawyer Atticus Finch, at the end of Harper Lee's novel *To Kill a Mockingbird*.[12] Atticus practices law in Maycomb, Alabama, and is the single parent of two young children. His nemesis, the villain of the story, Bob Ewell, tries to murder the children at night, when they are coming home from a school play. He is

---

[11] *See id.* at 146–47.

[12] *See* Lee, To Kill a Mockingbird, *supra* Chapter 3 note 7.

prevented from doing so by the intervention of a strange recluse named Boo Radley, who stabs and kills Bob Ewell.

Both Atticus and the sheriff understand what has happened. But the sheriff proposes to report to the town that Ewell fell on his own knife and to say nothing about Radley. He proposes to do this because he thinks it is better for the town and for the Radley family that Boo Radley remain a recluse. His purpose may be analogous to Irma's lawyer not telling the "whole truth" about her tavern-cleaning arrangement and saying, in his moral conversation with Irma, that it should not stand in the way of her getting S.S.I. (The soundness of Boo Radley's remaining a recluse is, however, not explored in Harper Lee's story, a question that shows how the lie-so-that-good-may-come reasoning takes on a heavy burden in deciding whether what may come is really good.)

Atticus at first objects to what the sheriff plans to do; they argue as they stand on the porch of the Finch home; and then Atticus changes his mind and agrees to the lie. He turns to his daughter, and asks her if she can understand what he is doing. She remembers Atticus's telling the children, when they got air rifles for Christmas, that it is a sin to kill a mockingbird. She says that telling the truth about Ewell's death would be like killing a mockingbird—thus giving the novel its title and carrying out its theme, which, Harper Lee said, was to tell the story of a conscience.

John Murray would no doubt (as he did in his book) quote John Calvin:

> [A]lthough our purpose be to assist our brethren, to consult for their safety and relieve them, it never can be lawful to lie, because that cannot be right which is contrary to the nature of God. And God is truth. And still the act . . . is not devoid of the praise of virtue, although it was not spotlessly pure. For it often happens that while the saints study to hold the right path, they deviate into circuitous courses.[13]

Witness Rebecca.

When *To Kill a Mockingbird* was made into a movie, the scene on the porch initially was developed in faithfulness to the novel. The movie was then reviewed by the National Legion of Decency, an agency of the Roman Catholic Church that reviewed movies for moral content. The Legion objected to the scene on the porch; the Legion proposed to give the movie a rating that meant "morally objectionable," because it showed a moral paragon telling a lie. Good Catholics did not go to "morally objectionable" movies.

The moviemakers changed the scene; as it appears now in the movie, Atticus does not endorse the sheriff's lie. He knows about it, but when he

---

[13] *See* Murray, *supra* Chapter 9 note 2, at 139, *quoting* John Calvin, Commentary, Joshua 2:4-6 (Henry Beveridge, trans, Grand Rapids, 1946).

asks his daughter if she understands, he is talking not about what he is doing but about what the sheriff is doing. The movie was fitted within the boundaries of the Legion's biblical reasoning; it received a rating of morally acceptable; and Gregory Peck (as Atticus Finch) won an Academy Award. It is perhaps a pleasant irony that Harper Lee received the Pulitzer Prize for telling the story the way the movie told it in the first place.

From the perspective of truthfulness as a virtue, there is a difference between looking at Atticus as a truthful person (which he certainly was) and an ethical judgment that turns on the content of his words. This argument says that the good habit (the virtue) of truthfulness is more important than the question of whether a particular act, taken in particular circumstances, was analytically right or wrong. For example, Atticus tipped his hat to the hateful and ugly old woman next door and told her she was as pretty as a picture.

Shirley Letwin, in studying the moral figure of the gentleman in Anthony Trollope's novels,[14] talked extensively of this virtue of truthfulness. She took up Kant's example of the killer who asks me which way his victim went. (Kant said I cannot lie, not even then.) She said, approving of the Trollopian gentleman, that he will lie to protect the victim; but, she added, because the Trollopian gentleman is a virtuous person, and his virtues include the virtue of truthfulness, he will not pretend that he has not lied.

The moral philosopher, Herbert Fingarette, seems to have depended on this sort of reasoning when he said, of the assertion (by one of your authors) that Atticus's behavior on the porch was a moral mistake:

> You wrongly treat the virtue of honesty and truthfulness in terms of an abstract principle to be understood as a logical universal. This seems to me to be incompatible with the spirit of responding to particular human beings, rather than living a moral life conceived ultimately in terms of abstract principle. I do not think the view I'm pushing here is merely a casuistical device for not noticing lies. Of course it is readily *used* in this way, by any of us. But then all things with the power of right are vulnerable to corruption in the service of evil. . . . Atticus's dilemma is that he, a man for whom truth is so central, is in this case doing right to forego "telling the truth." It is a humbling burden. It would be so satisfying if he could live a life of truthfulness by always telling the truth. No such luck. Truth is more mysterious.[15]

We agree with Fingarette that truthfulness is better seen as a virtue than as a principle, but we still believe that Atticus made a moral mistake. Our argument is that Atticus made a mistake in not telling the truth about

---

[14] *See* Shirley Letwin, The Gentleman in Trollope; Individuality and Moral Conduct (1982).

[15] *Quoted in* Shaffer, American Legal Ethics, *supra* Chapter 7 note 20, at 17.

the death of Bob Ewell because Atticus's motive for the lie was to protect Boo Radley from public notice. Atticus thought he had to protect the weak—including, to use a phrase of one of William Faulkner's Southern-gentleman lawyers, "the weak who are not even weak." We think it would have been better for Boo Radley to be out of doors. That would be the claim of modern advocates for mentally disabled people.

Our argument, that Atticus made a moral mistake, depends on noticing that admirable people whose ethic calls on them to protect the weak often deceive themselves. There may be an analogy between protecting Boo Radley and the argument, in Irma's case, that neither the letter nor the spirit of federal welfare law requires Irma to stay up all night, through painful periods of labor and rest, to clean a tavern. Maybe Irma's lawyer ought to discuss with Irma both the issue of the statements on the form and the issue of what she is to say to the judge, as, maybe, Atticus should have discussed with Boo Radley the adulation that would have come from neighbors knowing that Boo saved two lives. Self-deception is the risk one takes in telling a lie that good may come. This sort of self-deception is, as Atticus's story shows, peculiarly the risk of the person who means well.

All of this is background to a discussion of this issue of truthfulness between Irma and her lawyer—in terms of her conscience, in terms of his conscience, and in terms of a third conscience that such a moral conversation will produce. Here is the pre-hearing conversation between Irma and her lawyer:

* * *

Tom: Irma, I asked you to come in because we have word back from the administrative law judge assigned to your case. The judge is a lady named Markham; I have had cases in front of her before; she is a kind person and a good judge, but, of course, I don't know how she will decide your case.

Irma: Well, they already turned me down.

Tom: This is a new round, Irma. Judge Markham has not been involved in your case before. She is looking at it for the first time.

Irma: Well, I know I cannot work. I have told them. I am sick, all the time. I spend most days in bed. I can't work. That's what it's about, isn't it? Whether I can work?

Tom: Yes. What I want to do today is tell you a little bit about this hearing, which has been set for the fourteenth of next month, by the way. Then I want to talk about a couple of things that will come up.

Irma: Okay.

Tom: This is a real case, before a real judge. But it is pretty informal. Judge Markham will rent a room at Holiday Inn downtown and set up her court there. She won't wear a robe, but she will sit behind a table and talk to us. She will be a real judge, but won't look much like a judge on television. There will also be a person there to take notes for the judge. They will probably put it on a tape recorder. And there will probably be a person there who is an expert on jobs—to talk about what you can do and what jobs are available for you to do.

Irma: There aren't any jobs. I can't do any jobs.

Tom: Okay. But this person may say you can. We may have to argue about what he says you can do. There won't be anybody else there—no one from the Social Security Administration. It won't be like a trial with someone on the other side, except possibly for this vocational expert.

Irma: It doesn't matter what he says. I know what I can do.

Tom: Of course. And the judge will want to talk with you about that. She will want to ask you questions herself. She will probably let me ask you a few questions—about your surgery, and how you feel, about your shortness of breath, and what you do every day. But then she will want to talk with you herself, about those things.

Irma: All right. I will tell her.

Tom: Now, there are a couple of things I want to ask you about. One is this arrangement you have to clean the tavern downstairs.

Irma: Okay.

Tom: You may remember, Irma, that the form the lady at Social Security helped you fill out does not say anything about that work.

Irma: I thought it did.

Tom: No. It doesn't.

Irma: I'm pretty sure I told her about it. She asked me how I spend my days, and I told her, and I am pretty sure I told her about that.

Tom: Well, she didn't put anything about it in the form. After we talked about it earlier—you and I—I sent a letter to the judge about this. The letter says: "The applicant"—that's you—"gets consideration on the rent for her apartment by occasional help with cleaning the building in which she lives." I thought we ought to say something about it. That's why I sent the letter.

Irma: "Occasional"? It's not "occasional." I work down there every night—except Sundays. Harvey is closed on Sundays.

Tom: Is the work pretty hard for you?

Irma: Sure it's hard. Harvey has a little cot in the back that I can rest on. But—sure—it's very hard. It takes me hours to do.

Tom: Do you think it harms your health?

Irma: My health is terrible to begin with. But, yes, it harms my health.

Tom: Your health would be better, and you would feel better, if you didn't have to do it.

Irma: Yes. Read that again. What does it say?

Tom: It says, "The applicant gets consideration on the rent for her apartment by occasional help with cleaning the building in which she lives." Do you think that is the truth?

Irma: No. It's not. What I do down there is not "occasional." I want to tell the truth. Why shouldn't I? What does "consideration" mean?

Tom: It means you get money taken off your rent.

Irma: I don't pay any rent. I can't pay any rent. If Harvey didn't help me out, I don't know what I would do. I would not have any place to live.

Tom: So he is helping you out. Not really hiring you to do work.

Irma: Oh, I do plenty of work. It's very hard.

Tom: Well, there are a couple of ways we can talk about that, if we talk with the judge about it at all. The thing I was thinking, as a lawyer does, is that if we keep the issue simple it is easier to win the case. And I wondered whether we ought to say anything about this cleaning work. If we don't say anything, the judge may still ask about it. What will you say if she asks you about it?

Irma: I will tell her the truth—what I do, how hard it is, and what I get for it.

Tom: You would want to tell her the whole story.

Irma: Sure I would.

Tom: I wonder whether we ought to go in and just tell her about it at first. When I sent this letter, I thought "occasional" and "consideration" were the right words—that they were the truth. But I guess they weren't.

Irma: No.

Tom: So—you think we ought to go in there and tell her our story.

Irma: Well, you're the lawyer—

Tom: But you want to tell the truth, right up front—all of it?

Irma: Yes.

Tom: All right. That's what we'll do.

Conclusion

■ ■ ■

People become lawyers for many reasons. For some it is for money; for some it is the thrill of competition and a desire for success; for others it is the status that comes from being in a profession. But the big desk, the plaques on the walls, and the things that one can purchase with a large income can carry a person only so far. We suspect that part of the reason that many lawyers are disenchanted with the practice of law is that these things are not inherently satisfying.

Maybe we need a new vision of law practice—or the revival of an old vision. At its root, being a lawyer is helping people. Sometimes those people come in with their own problems; sometimes they are part of an organization that has problems. The most meaningful times in the practice of law come from helping people. The deepest and most important way we can help them is when we help them to become better people. Robert Whitfield, who helped his client to settle a dispute with his son-in-law, illustrates the satisfaction that this type of practice brings. Whitfield hopes the settlement will enable the client, his son-in-law, his daughter, and his grandchildren to be reconciled. Whitfield says: "I have accomplished nothing more satisfying in the ten years of my practice than this. If I were not paid a penny for the work, I would have no complaint."[1]

The exciting side of such a practice derives from the belief—which, we trust, we share with our readers—that people, including clients, are an adventure. Each of them, in an unexpected and even miraculous way, can be a joy. We disagree with the character in Sartre's play who said that Hell is other people—lawyers who think so are unlikely to enjoy practice (or anything else). Those who see other people, including clients, as a gift are likely to agree with Martin Buber, who says, "I become aware of him, aware that he is different from myself, in the definite, unique way which is peculiar to him, and I accept whom I thus see. . . . I can recognize in him, know in him, more or less, the person he has been (I can say it only in this word) created to become."[2] If this book helps lawyers to relate to clients in this way, we will be pleased.

---

1 Jack & Jack, Moral Vision and Professional Decisions, *supra* Chapter 1 note 32, at 92.

2 Buber, The Knowledge of Man, *supra* Chapter 4 note 28, at 171–72.

INDEX

References are to Pages